Math Lesson 2

A Place

SonLight Education Ministry
United States of America

A Suggested Daily Schedule

(Adapt this schedule to your family needs.)

5:00 a.m.   Arise–Personal Worship

6:00 a.m.   Family Worship and Bible Class–With Father

7:00 a.m.   Breakfast

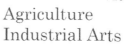

8:00 a.m.   Practical Arts*–Domestic Activities
                                               Agriculture
                                               Industrial Arts
                                               (especially those related to
                                               the School Lessons)

10:00 a.m.   School Lessons
                           (Take a break for some physical exercise
                           during this time slot.)

12:00 p.m.   Dinner Preparations
                           (Health class could be included at this time
                           or a continued story.)

1:00 p.m.   Dinner

2:00 p.m.   Practical Arts* or Fine Arts
                           (Music and Crafts)
                           (especially those related to
                           the School Lessons)

5:00 p.m.   Supper

6:00 p.m.   Family Worship–Father
                           (Could do History Class)

7:00 p.m.   Personal time with God–Bed Preparation

8:00 p.m.   Bed

*Daily nature walk can be in morning or afternoon.

The Desire of All Nations

This book is a part of a curriculum that is built upon the life of Christ entitled, "The Desire of All Nations," for grades 2-8. Any of the books in this curriculum can be used by themselves or as an entire program.

INFORMATION ABOUT THE 2-8 GRADE PROGRAM

Multi-level

This program is written on a multi-level. That means that each booklet has material for grades 2-8. This is so the whole family in these grades may work from the same books. It is difficult for a busy mother to have 2 or more children and each have a different set of books. Remember, the Bible is written for all ages.

The Bible—the Primary Textbook

The books in this program are designed to teach the parent and the student how to learn academic subjects by using the Bible as a primary textbook.

The Desire of Ages

The Desire of Ages by Ellen G. White is used as a textbook to go with the Bible. This focuses on the early life of Christ, when He was a child. Children relate best to Christ as a child and youth.

Lesson Numbers

The big number in the top right corner on the cover of this book is the Lesson Number and corresponds with the chapter number in the book *The Desire of Ages*. For example, Lesson 1 in the school program will go along with chapter 1 in *The Desire of Ages*. Usually each family starts at the beginning with Lesson 1. Most children have not had a true Bible program, therefore they need the foundation built. If there is academic material that they have already covered, they do the Bible part and review then pass quickly on.

Seven Academic Subjects

There are seven academic subjects in this program—Health, Mathematics, Music, Science–Nature, History/Geography/Prophecy, Language, Voice–Speech.

Language Program

A good, solid language program is recommended to be used along with the SonLight materials.

The Riggs Institute has a multi-sensory teaching method that accommodates every child's unique learning style. Their program is called *Writing and Spelling Road to Reading and Thinking*. Order by calling (800) 200-4840 or visit www.riggsinst.org. (Disclaimer: SonLight does not endorse the reading books recommended in the Riggs' program.)

Another option which you might find more user friendly and is similar to the Riggs program but from a Christian perspective is *Spell to Write and Read* by Wanda Sanseri. To order, call Wanda Sanseri at (503) 654-2300 or visit https://www.bhibooks.net/swr.html

"God's Chosen People"
Lesson 2 – Diligence

The following books are those you will need for this lesson.
All of these can be obtained from www.sonlighteducation.com

The Rainbow Covenant – Study the spiritual meaning of colors and make your own rainbow book.

Health
The Body

Math
A Place

Music
What Makes Sound?

Science/Nature
The Universe and Galaxies

A Casket – Coloring book and story. Learn how to treat the gems of the Bible.

H/G/P
The Earth

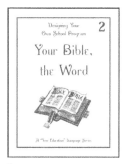

Language
Your Bible, the Word

Speech/Voice
Care of the Voice

Spelling from the Scriptures

Bible Study – Learn how to study the Bible and helpful use tools.

Bible
The Desire of all Nations I
Teacher Study Guide

Student Study Guide

Bible Lesson Study Guide

Memory Verses
The Desire of all Nations I
Scripture Songs Book
and MP3 files

Our Nature Study Book – Your personal nature journal.

Instructions

1. Work through the sections that your child can do. Each section becomes increasingly harder. Just because a section is marked for a certain level do not stop there if your student can move on through more mature material. (Place I – Ones/Tens/Hundreds • Place II – Hundreds/Thousands • Place III – Thousands/Millions/Billions)

2. If your child needs extra help, the teacher can make more problems by using the Bible, nature, or the other lessons.

3. **Bible Lesson**: *"The Chosen People"* (*The Desire of Ages*, pages 27-30)— Keep bringing the child's mind back to this lesson during your daily living. If you need reminders, write on a 3 by 5 card some ideas and carry them with you through the day.

Memory Verses: Deuteronomy 4:5-6
Deuteronomy 28:10
Deuteronomy 26:18-19
Isaiah 56:7

When waking, going for walks, riding in the car, working in the kitchen, or whatever, have your student repeat his memory verses.

Character Quality: **Diligence** – constant effort to accomplish what is undertaken; exertion of body or mind without unnecessary delay or sloth; due attention; industry.

Use every daily opportunity to teach your student **diligence**. We are told: *"They that sow in tears shall reap in joy"* (Psalm 126:5). Think about the following thoughts. "By labor fire is got out of a stone." —*Dutch Proverb*

"Elbow-grease is the best polish." —*English Proverb*

"Few things are impossible to **diligence** and skill." —*Samuel Johnson* (1759)

Dictionary of Terms

digit – any of the numerals 1 to 9 and the symbol 0.

chosen – selected or marked for favor or special privilege as chosen by God.

lose sight – to be unable to find or see.

place – the position of a numeral in relation to others of a series and especially of a numeral to the right of a decimal point.

ones' place – one digit

tens' place – two digits

hundreds' place – three digits

thousands' place – four, five, and six digits

millions' place – seven, eight, or nine digits

billions' place – ten, eleven, twelve digits

value – the worth, usefulness, or importance of something (like numbers, people, especially you.)

Table of Contents

Instructions	**Page i**
Teacher Section	**Pages 1-28**
Student Section	**Pages 1-72**
Research	
Place Value—Ones and Tens	Page 1
Placed	Page 1
Reflect	Page 1
Reflect	Page 2
Review – Ones and Tens	Page 3
God/Israel – Illustration	Page 3
Reflect	Page 4
"Diligent Worker" – Story	Page 4
Remarkable Facts	Page 5
Research	
A Special Place	Page 6
Reinforce – Serve	Page 6
A Map of Israel Today – Illustration	Page 6
"Diligent Workers" – Stories	Page 6
Review	Page 7
Research	
Serving Self	Page 8
Review	Page 8
"Others Not Self" – Story	Page 8
Reflect	Page 9
Research	
Trials	Page 9
Review	Page 10
Reflect	Page 10

Table of Contents

Research
  Sacrifices and Ceremonies   Page 11
    Review   Page 11
    Reflect   Page 11

Research
  Heavy Burdens   Page 12
    Review   Page 13
    Remarkable Facts   Page 13

Research
  Waiting   Page 14
    Review   Page 15
    Reinforce   Page 15
      "Watching" – Story   Page 16

Research
  Writing the Bible   Page 17
    Review   Page 17
      "The Bible A Treasure" – Story   Page 18
    Reflect – Bible Authorship is Wonderful   Page 18

Research
  Work   Page 19
    Reinforce   Page 19
    Reinforce   Page 20
      "Planned" – Poem   Page 20
      "**Diligent** Work" – Story   Page 20
    Review   Page 21
    Review   Page 26
    Reflect   Page 27
    Reinforce   Page 28
      "Work Should Begin Early" – Story   Page 28
    Remind   Page 28

Table of Contents

Research
  Place Value—Hundreds   Page 29
    The Bible   Page 29
      Reflect   Page 29
      Reinforce   Page 30
        "Knowledge of the Bible" – Story   Page 30
        "The Bible Adapted to Our Daily Lives" – Information   Page 30
      Review   Page 31
      Reflect   Page 31
      Reflect – **"Diligence"**   Page 32
      Reflect – The Law   Page 34

Research
    The Right Place   Page 35
      Reinforce   Page 35
        "Right Place At the Right Time" – Story   Page 35
      Review   Page 36
        "In the Right Place to Hear the Word" – Story   Page 36
      Remarkable Facts   Page 37
      Reinforce   Page 38
        "Work Can Be Fun!" – Story   Page 38
      Review   Page 39
      Reflect   Page 40
      Reinforce   Page 40

Research
  Place Value—Thousands, Ten Thousands, Hundred Thousands   Page 41
    Chosen   Page 41
      Reflect   Page 41
        "Choice" – Story   Page 42
      Review   Page 43

Table of Contents

Research
  Set Apart .... Page 44
    Reflect .... Page 44
      "Every Little Light" – Poem .... Page 44
      "Diligently Work" – Thought .... Page 44
    Review .... Page 46
    Reinforce .... Page 49
    Remind .... Page 50
    Review .... Page 50
    Reflect .... Page 50

Research
  Valuable .... Page 51
    Reflect – Gold of Ophir .... Page 52
    Remind .... Page 52
    Review .... Page 53
    Reflect – Value .... Page 54

Research
  Place Value—Millions/Ten Millions/Hundred Millions/Billions/Ten Billions/Hundred Billions ... Page 55
  Lost Sight .... Page 55
    Digital Value and Place Value – Examples ... Page 56
    Reflect – Sight .... Page 56
    Reflect .... Page 57
    Reinforce .... Page 58
      "Seeing Eyes" – Story .... Page 58
      "All Seeing Eyes" – Story .... Page 58
    Reflect – Precious In My Sight .... Page 59
      "God Made Them All" – Poem .... Page 59
    Review .... Page 60
    Reinforce .... Page 60
      "Eyes and No Eyes" – Story .... Page 60
      "Seeing the Light" – Thought .... Page 60
    Reflect – We See Light, Harmony, and Beauty.... Page 62

Table of Contents

Remainder

The Eyes of the Lord — Page 62
    Review — Page 63
        "God's Care for You" – Poem — Page 63
    Remind — Page 64
    Reinforce — Page 64
    Review — Page 65
    More Review — Page 66
        Place Value – Illustration — Page 69
    Review — Page 70
    Reflect — Page 70
        "Place" – Mark Your Bible — Page 71

"And speak unto him [Joshua], saying,
Thus speaketh the Lord of hosts, saying,
Behold the man whose name is the BRANCH [Christ];
and he shall grow up [to spring forth] out of his place,
and he shall build the temple [spiritual house] of the Lord."
Zechariah 6:12

Teacher Section

"Even unto them will I give
in mine house and within my walls
a place and a name
better than of sons and of daughters."
Isaiah 56:5

INSTRUCTIONS
For the Teacher

Step 1

Study the Bible Lesson and begin to memorize the Memory Verses. Familiarize yourself with the Character Quality. The student can answer the Bible Review Questions. See page 10. Use the Steps in Bible Study.

Bible Lesson

God's Chosen People – Exodus 20:3-6; Psalm 115:4-8; Isaiah 43:10, 11; 49:3-6; 56:7; Ezra 9:5-7; Romans 1:22-23

Memory Verses

Isaiah 56:7; Deuteronomy 26:18-19; 28:10; 4:5-6

Character Quality

Diligence – constant effort to accomplish what is undertaken; exertion of body or mind without unnecessary delay or sloth; due attention; industry.

Antonyms – dilatoriness; slowness; casualness; slothfulness

Character Quality Verses

Colossians 3:23 – *"And whatsoever ye do, do it heartily, as to the Lord, and not unto men."*

Proverbs 4:23 –*"Keep thy heart with all **diligence**; for out of it are the issues of life."*

Step 2

Understand How To/And

A. Do the spelling cards so the student can begin to build his own spiritual dictionary.

B. How to Mark Your Bible.

C. Evaluate Your Student's Character in relation to the character quality of **diligence**.

D. Familiarize Yourself With "A Place." Notice the Projects.

E. Review the Scripture references for "A Place."

F. Notice the Answer Key.

A. Spelling Cards

Spelling Lists

Math Words
Place I - II- III
burdens
choice
chosen
digital
eye(s)
heavy
lost
place
placed
position
precious
right
sight
trials
value
waiting
watching
worker
worth
writing
(Place I should
be able to spell
the numbers
1-12.)

Place II- III
billions
ceremonies
hardships
hundreds

humiliation
millions
sacrifices
separated
serving
thousands
tribulations

Bible Words
Place I - II - III
chosen
covenant
diligence
diligent
diligently
fools
glorified
graven
idols
image
iniquities
jealous
light
likeness
professing
restore
servant
serve
trespass
witnesses
wise

B. How to Mark Your Bible

1. Copy the list of Bible texts in the back of the Bible on an empty page as a guide.

2. Go to the first text in the Bible and copy the next text beside it. Go to the next one and repeat the process until they are all chain-referenced.

3. Have the student present the study to family and/or friends.

4. In each student lesson there is one or more sections that have a Bible marking study on the subject studied. (See the Student's Section, pages 71-72.)

C. Evaluate Your Student's Character

This section is for the purpose of helping the teacher to know how to encourage the students to become more **diligent**.

See page 11.

> **See the booklet**
> ***Spelling from the Scriptures***
> **for instructions about how to make the Spelling Cards.**

D. Familiarize Yourself With "A Place" – Notice the Projects

Projects

1. Help your child learn his place in the home to become a **diligent** son or daughter. Help him learn his value in God's sight—He even sent His Son to redeem him.

2. As you work in the kitchen or go shopping be aware of the value of numbers and their place in your everyday life.

3. Notice the starry sky on a clear night. Discuss the value of each one of these lights in God's great universe. Find Bible verses that refer to these stars or suns.

4. Discuss the church and how certain people have been chosen to fill different places of responsibility in the church. How about in the home? In the community? In the government?

5. Each child choose a friend and share the concepts that are being learned in this lesson. Do this by letter or in person.

6. Take a nature walk and find several things in nature that have a place, then parallel it with your Bible lesson and the character quality of **diligence**. Use *Our Nature Study Book*.

(Example: A tree has a set place. The tree occupies the place God has put it. Israel had a set place assigned to them. They were not **diligent** in occupying their place nor did they value their own worth and advantages.)

7. Read and explain Matthew 10:31.

8. Read together Isaiah 13:12. How does this verse relate to our Bible story, "God's Chosen People?" Record your discussion so each can evaluate how well they express themselves.

9. Clean your room and find a place for all of your things.

10. On the next 4 pages are additional stories and poems to use when appropriate.

> **Placement of Student**
> **Place I = Grades 2-3-4**
> **Place II = Grades 4-5-6**
> **Place III = Grades 6-7-8**

A Sensible Suggestion

"If I could only be of some use in the world, or fill some <u>place</u> in it," cried Frances, impatiently, "I would not complain."

"Well," suggested Cousin Patty, "making beds is very useful work, and your mother seems to need some one to fill the <u>place</u> of mender-in-ordinary to the family. Why not begin where you are? I never saw anybody willing to be of use who couldn't be used right where he stood. And as for filling places—did you ever think that you are put in your own <u>place</u> so as to fill it? This business of wanting to climb out of your own <u>place</u> before you've filled it, to go hunting for an empty one somewhere else, never did seem sensible to me. Start right in to be of use, and you'll be useful, never fear."

It was a sensible suggestion. There are many useless people excusing themselves today by saying that they would rejoice to be of use somewhere else. Our own <u>place</u>, after all, is the only one we can ever fill. The moment we fill it full, we shall overflow it into wider bounds. Mending and making beds, running errands, doing chores—the large careers begin by these small use-fulnesses, and widen irrepressibly as the man and the woman develop into broader activities. "Begin where you are" is common sense. As a matter of fact, we can develop what we shall be—only from where we stand can the first forward step be made. Shirking and complaining belong together. They are a poor pair of twins to have about, and the sooner we turn them out of doors, and determine to be **alert** and thoroughly useful in our own present <u>place</u>, the better.

—Well Spring

An Incident for the Boys

At the head of an important department in one of the great stores in New York City is a man with an interesting history. His career affords a fine illustration of the kind of spirit that wins in the business world of today. Only a few years ago he appeared at this store as an applicant for a position. "No place for you," gruffly said the manager. "But I've got to have a place," persisted the man. "My family will starve unless I get something to do. Look at me. Things have gone against me, but through no fault of mine. Am I a decent-looking fellow?" "Yes, you are," replied the manager, "but I have no place which I can give you."

"But my wife and children are dependent upon me, and will soon be at the point of suffering unless I get work. Is there not some way in which I could be useful, and for which I could receive a sufficient amount with which to buy bread at least?" There was an earnestness of voice that made its appeal. "What are you willing to do?" said the manager. "Anything and everything," replied our friend. "Well, I suppose I could give you a place as sort of lackey boy. You will have to do plenty of work, some of it very disagreeable, and your pay will be but six dollars a week." "All right, sir, I'll take the job, and I thank you for it."

Thus humbly did he begin. He studied to make himself useful. He was one of the first to be on hand in the morning, and often lingered after close of hours to put everything in perfect order for the next day. He did not wait to be told what to do. He could not have taken a livelier interest had he been one of the proprietors. In a short time promotion came. After a few months he was put in charge of a delivery route. Some way he found time to do extra work. Every day he brought in new orders for goods. The increase of trade on his route attracted attention. Little by little he won his way until he was placed at the head of a most important department. For several years he has drawn a salary of eighteen thousand dollars a year. How silly the cry that there are no opportunities for young men in business! There were never better opportunities than now. Push, pluck, and a right spirit are the great needs, and are sure to win.

—*William F. Anderson,*
in Epworth Herald.

Quality, Not Place

Said A, "Whene'er I stand between
    The letters B and D,
I'm in the midst of all that's BaD,
    As you can plainly see."

"How strange!" said merry, laughing E,
    "When I between them am,
I'm tucked up comfortably in BeD,
    And happy as a clam."

"It's quality within ourselves,"
    Then mused the letter A,
"And not the <u>place</u> we occupy,
    That makes us sad or gay."
        —Nicholas

A Place

It was Johnny, the seven-year-old, who tired of the "merry-go-round." The previous summer it had fascinated him, and he could not ride on it too often; this season a single trip satisfied him, and he declined another. "No, thank you, grandfather," he said, in his quaintly polite way. "You see we ride and ride, but we stay under that old tent all the time. I guess when anybody gets to be seven years old, he's too big to care about going and going that doesn't get anywhere."

"Now, may the boy hold fast to his wisdom!" commented the grandfather, relating the incident. "Selecting a goal and traveling toward it would seem to be a reasonable theory of existence, but there are plenty of grown-ups who are content to spend a lifetime in the sort of 'going and going that never gets anywhere.' I don't know that it matters much whether it is an occupation, or society, or only a childish merry-go-round that carries us, if we are content with the mere round, and seek no worthy destination."
—*Selected*

One Spot

God gives all men all earth to love,
But, since man's heart is small,
Ordains for each one spot shall prove
Beloved over all.
—*Rudyard Kipling*

"The lowly <u>places</u>
are the holy <u>places</u>."
—*The Youth Instructor* 613

E. Review the Scripture References for "A Place"

Teacher, read through this section before working on the lesson with the student.

See pages 71-72 in the Student Section.

F. Notice the Answer Key

The Answer key for the student book is found on page 12.

Step 3

Read the Lesson Aim.

Lesson Aim

The purpose of this lesson is: to teach the child the definition of place value and digital value; to help the child make spiritual parallels from the Bible lesson and the Nature lesson; to teach the child place value, to teach the child how to write numbers out; to teach the child his place, to teach the child the value of that place as God designed; to encourage him to be **diligent** in all his responsibilities.

"To His servants Christ commits *'His goods'*—something to be put to use for Him. He gives *'to every man his work.'* Each has his place in the eternal plan of heaven. Each is to work in co-operation with Christ for the salvation for souls. Not more surely in the place prepared for us in the heavenly mansions than is the special place designated on earth where we are to work for God." (*Christ's Object Lessons* 326-327)

God had designed a place for His people, the children of Israel. They were the ones through whom the Messiah would come to this earth. They were to help prepare the world for His first advent. The children of Israel were to be **diligent** in their responsibility. Were they?

God designed a place for each galaxy. He designed a place for this world to fill in the massive universe. He designed a place for each member of your family to fill. Jesus is coming again. Will you take your place and be **diligent** in helping to prepare others for this event? And then like the people in Acts 2:1 *"...They were all with one accord in one place."*

Step 4

Prepare to begin the "A Place" Lesson.

To Begin The "A Place" Lesson

Make a list of each family member and the place they have in the family. Next, list the order of place in the heavenly family. Finally, discover the place you will have someday in heaven!

Step 5

These lessons are designed for the whole family. Begin "A Place" lesson. Cover only what can be understood by your student. Make the lessons a family project by involving everyone in part or all of the studies.

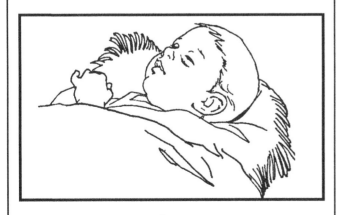

Steps in Bible Study

1. Prayer

2. Read the verses/meditate/memorize.

3. Look up key words in *Strong's Concordance* and find their meanings in the Hebrew or Greek dictionary in the back of that book.

4. Cross reference (marginal reference) with other Bible texts. An excellent study tool is *The Treasury of Scripture Knowledge.*

5. Use Bible custom books for more information on the times.

6. Write a summary of what you have learned from those verses.

7. Mark key thoughts in the margin of your Bible.

8. Share your study with others to reinforce the lessons you have learned.

Review Questions

1. What religious worship prevailed in ancient times? (Romans 1:22-23; Psalm 115:4-8)

2. What was the great mission of the chosen people, Israel? (Exodus 20:3-6; Isaiah 43:10, 11; 49:3-6; 56:7)

3. How did they fail in their duty? (Ezra 9:5-7)

4. Thought Question: How did God overrule Israel's failure for the accomplishment of His purpose and their mission?

5. What three nations or races were most influential in the civilized world at the time of Christ? For what was each remarkable? (a. Rome–Law; b. Greeks–Language; c. Jews–Religion)

6. What had each contributed to prepare the way for the spread of the gospel? (a. Rome – Government; b. Greek – Language; c. Jews – Knowledge of the true God)

7. God prepared the Gentile world for the coming of the Redeemer by:

a. Causing the system of heathenism to lose its hold on the people;

b. Translating the Bible into Greek, which was the universal language;

c. Having a remnant of Jews who were steadfast to the true God; and

d. Allowing Palestine to be the center of the world's gatherings.

8. Who are God's chosen people today? Who are His faithful followers?

Questions 5, 6 and 7 will need to be asked and then answered by the teacher.

Evaluating Your Child's Character

Check the appropriate box for your student's level of development,
or your own, as the case may be.

Maturing Nicely (MN), Needs Improvement (NI), Poorly Developed (PD), Absent (A)

Diligence

1. Does the student have difficulty in following through on assigned tasks without being reminded?

Yes ☐ **No** ☐

2. Does the student tend to take on the responsibilities of others, leaving his own responsibilities unattended?

Yes ☐ **No** ☐

3. Is the student able to complete tasks in spite of distractions?

Yes ☐ **No** ☐

4. Does the student need constant supervision in order to perform at his best level?

Yes ☐ **No** ☐

5. Is the time that a child can wait between achievement and reward increasing appreciably?

MN ☐ **NI** ☐ **PD** ☐ **A** ☐

6. Does the student move quickly and efficiently on the job, or does he move slowly?

MN ☐ **NI** ☐ **PD** ☐ **A** ☐

7. Does the student look forward to the job or complains about the task?

MN ☐ **NI** ☐ **PD** ☐ **A** ☐

8. Will the student first do the job to please the Lord and then his parents?

MN ☐ **NI** ☐ **PD** ☐ **A** ☐

Answer Key

Page 2

Trials = humiliation, tribulations, and hardships, trouble, misery, and affliction

Page 3

12

Page 4

(1) 1, 1, 2, 2
     1, 2, 2, 2
     1, 2, 2, 2
     1, 1, 2, 2
     1, 1, 2, 2

(2) 12
     1
     2
     1, 2
     1, 2
     12, 1, 2

Page 5

1st generation	268
2nd generation	1,072
3rd generation	4,288
4th generation	17,152
5th generation	68,608
6th generation	274,432
7th generation	1,097,728 males
	1,097,728 females
Total	2,195,456

Page 7

1, 3, 12
(1) 1 one
(2) 3 three
(3) 12 twelve

Page 8

1, 7, 10

Page 9

(1) 1 one
(2) 7 seven
(3) 10 ten

Page 10

9, 11, 6

(1) 9 nine
(2) 11 eleven
(3) 6 six

Page 11

Mullitudinous = consisting of a multitude or great number. Extravagant = one who is confined to no general rule or limits
8, 5, 4

Page 12 (1) 8 eight
          (2) 5 five
          (3) 4 four

Answer Key

Page 13   constant effort to accomplish what is undertaken; exertion of body or mind without unnecessary delay or slothfulness; due attention; industry

Israel wanted to be important in this world. They **diligently** served themselves instead of **diligently** making Jesus most important in their lives and in the lives of others.

13,500 days; 135,000 working hours; 90,000 working hours

Page 15

66, 39, 27

(1)   66 sixty-six
(2)   39 thirty-nine
(3)   27 twenty-seven

Page 16

(4)   9
         9 nine
         9
         9 nine
(5)   18 eighteen

Page 17

40, forty
30, thirty
8, eight
50, fifty
39, thirty-nine
27, twenty-seven

Notes

Answer Key

Page 18		4, 0
		3, 0
		8
		5, 0
		3, 9
		2, 7
Page 21	(1)	L, L, L
		G, L, G
		G, G, L
		G, L, G
	(2)	0 - zero
Page 22		1 - one
		2 - two
		3 - three
Page 23		4 - four
		5 - five
		6 - six
Page 24		7 - seven
		8 - eight
		9 - nine
Page 25		10 - ten
		11 - eleven
		12 - twelve
Page 26	(1)	ones'
	(2)	tens' and ones'
	(3)	see right of this page

Page 26 continued

(4) zero
     one
     two
     three
     four
     five
     six
     seven
     eight
     nine

Tens	Ones
	1
	2
	3
	4
	5
	6
	7
	8
	9
1	0
1	1
1	2
2	7
3	9
6	6
1	8
4	0
3	0
5	0

Answer Key

Page 27

    ten
    eleven
    twelve
(5) 3, 5
    2, 2
    1, 1
    4, 6
    5, 3
    6, 6
    9, 1
    7, 5
    6, 4

(6) thirty-nine
    twenty-seven
    sixty-six

Page 31

(1) 9
    3, tens'
    ones'
(2) hundreds', 6
    ones'

Page 32

(3) 3
(4) 2
(5) 1
(6) 150, 0, 5, 1
(7) 66 + 52 = 118
    8, 1, 1

Page 33

Commandment	Hundreds	Tens	Ones
1			8
2		9	1
3		2	7
4		9	4
Total	2	2	4

Commandment	Hundreds	Tens	Ones
5		2	2
6			4
7			5
8			4
9			9
10		3	3
Total		7	7

Page 34

    297

Page 36

(1) place
    digital
(2) It tells you whether a digit is in the ones', tens', or hundreds' place.

Page 37

(3)   It tells how many ones', how many tens', how many hundreds'.

(4)   2, 2, 0
       0, 7, 7
       2, 9, 7
       1, 1, 9
       1, 7, 6
       1, 1, 7

Page 38

       6, 0, 0
       4, 0, 6
       4, 0, 4
       1, 0, 3

Page 39

(1)   hundreds'
       3

(2)   ⑦42 ⑦⑦2 166 ⑦89

       48⑦ 269 34⑦ 666

       5⑦6 3⑦2 292 ⑦⑦⑦

H	HT	_	H
O	_	O	_
T	T	_	HTO

H = Hundreds'
T = Tens'
O = Ones'

Page 40

(3)   two
       place
       digital

(4)   one
       two
       three
       four
       five
       six
       seven
       eight
       nine
       ten
       eleven
       twelve

(2)

H	T	O
7	4	2
7	7	2
1	6	6
7	6	9
4	8	7
2	6	9
3	4	7
6	6	6
5	7	6
3	7	2
2	9	2
7	7	7

Answer Key

Page 43   (1)

Milky Way Galaxy					
	ten thousands	thousands	hundreds	tens	ones
thickness		3	0	0	0
diameter	3	0	0	0	0

three thousand
thirty thousand

Thought for the Teacher

"All heaven is interested in the work going on in this world, which is to prepare men and women for the future, immortal life. It is God's plan that human agencies shall have the high honor of acting as co-workers with Jesus Christ in the salvation of souls. The word of God plainly reveals that it is the privilege of the instrument in this great work to realize that there is One at his right hand ready to aid him in every sincere endeavor to reach the highest moral and spiritual excellence in the Master's work. This will be the case with all who feel their need of help. They should look upon the work of God as sacred and holy, and should bring to Him, every day, offerings of joy and gratitude, in return for the power of His grace, by which they are enabled to make advancement in the divine life. The worker should ever take humble views of himself, considering his many lost opportunities for want of **diligence** and appreciation of the work. He should not become discouraged, but should continually renew his efforts to redeem the time."

—5 Testimonies 573-574

Answer Key

Page 46   (1)

Galaxy	distance /diameter	hundred thousands	ten thousands	one thousands	hundreds	tens	ones
Milky Way	distance						
"	diameter		3	0,	0	0	0
Large Mag	distance		4	8,	0	0	0
"	diameter		1	0,	0	0	0
Small Mag	distance		5	6,	0	0	0
"	diameter			8,	0	0	0
Ursa Minor	distance		7	0,	0	0	0
"	diameter			1,	0	0	0
Sculptor	distance		8	3,	0	0	0
"	diameter			2,	2	0	0
Draco	distance	1	0	0,	0	0	0
"	diameter			1,	4	0	0
Fornax	distance	1	9	0,	0	0	0
"	diameter			6,	6	0	0
Leo II	distance	2	3	0,	0	0	0
"	diameter			1,	6	0	0

Answer Key

Galaxy	distance/diameter	hundred thousands	ten thousands	one thousands	hundreds	tens	ones
Leo I	distance	2	8	0,	0	0	0
"	diameter			1,	5	0	0
NGC6822	distance	4	6	0,	0	0	0
"	diameter			2,	7	0	0
NGC147	distance	5	7	0,	0	0	0
"	diameter			3,	0	0	0
NGC185	distance	5	7	0,	0	0	0
"	diameter			2,	3	0	0
NGC205	distance	6	8	0,	0	0	0
"	diameter			5,	0	0	0
NGC221	distance	6	8	0,	0	0	0
"	diameter			2,	4	0	0
IC1613	distance	6	8	0,	0	0	0
"	diameter			5,	0	0	0
Andromeda	distance	6	8	0,	0	0	0
"	diameter		4	0,	0	0	0
NGC	distance	7	2	0,	0	0	0
"	diameter		1	7,	0	0	0

Answer Key

Page 48

Galaxy	distance /diameter	Write out appropriate number
Milky Way	distance	We are in the Milky Way galaxy
"	diameter	thirty thousand
Large Mag	distance	forty-eight thousand
"	diameter	ten thousand
Small Mag	distance	fifty-six thousand
"	diameter	eight thousand
Ursa Minor	distance	seventy thousand
"	diameter	one thousand
Sculptor	distance	eighty-three thousand
"	diameter	two thousand two hundred
Draco	distance	one hundred thousand
"	diameter	one thousand four hundred
Fornax	distance	one hundred ninety thousand
"	diameter	six thousand six hundred
Leo II	distance	two hundred thirty thousand
"	diameter	one thousand six hundred
Leo I	distance	two hundred eighty thousand
"	diameter	one thousand five hundred

Answer Key

Page 48 continued

Galaxy	distance /diameter	Write out appropriate number
NGC6822	distance	four hundred sixty thousand
"	diameter	two thousand seven hundred

Page 49

Galaxy	distance /diameter	Write out appropriate number
NGC147	distance	five hundred seventy thousand
"	diameter	three thousand
NGC185	distance	five hundred seventy thousand
"	diameter	two thousand three hundred
NGC205	distance	six hundred eighty thousand
"	diameter	five thousand
NGC221	distance	six hundred eighty thousand
"	diameter	two thousand four hundred
IC1613	distance	six hundred eight thousand
"	diameter	five thousand
Andromeda	distance	six hundred eighty thousand
"	diameter	forty thousand

Answer Key

Page 49 continued

Galaxy	distance /diameter	Write out appropriate number
NGC	distance	seven hundred twenty thousand
"	diameter	seventeen thousand

Page 53
(1) thousands'
(2) ten thousands'
(3) hundred thousands'
(4) see chart below

hundred thousands	ten thousands	one thousands'	hundreds'	tens'	ones'
				6	2
		7	6	5	8
	3	4	6	1	3
7	3	2	5	5	1
		2	2	7	1
	7	3	8	1	8
3	1	8	3	6	4
			3	0	6
	1	3	1	2	9
	6	1	8	3	2
9	5	4	6	2	3

Notes

Answer Key

Page 54   (5)   sixty-two
seven thousand, six hundred fifty-eight
thirty-four thousand, six hundred thirteen
seven hundred thirty-two thousand, five hundred fifty-one
two hundred seventy-two
two thousand, two hundred seventy-one
seventy-three thousand, eight hundred eighteen
three hundred eighteen thousand, three hundred sixty-four
three hundred six
thirteen thousand, one hundred twenty-nine
sixty-one thousand, eight hundred thirty-two
nine hundred fifty-four thousand, six hundred twenty-three

   (6)

	hundred thousands	ten thousands	one thousands'	hundreds'	tens'	ones'
A.			5	4	4	7
B.			3	1	8	2
C.			1	3	2	9
D.		5	0	9	2	1
E.		6	3	6	0	2
F.		2	4	8	6	9
G.	2	4	0	6	0	1
H.	4	3	9	5	3	6
I.	7	6	3	2	1	3

Notes

Answer Key

Page 54 (7)
continued

1,715
325
243,316
47
9,408
65,307
948,106
38,977
26,701
84,600
2,347
336,862

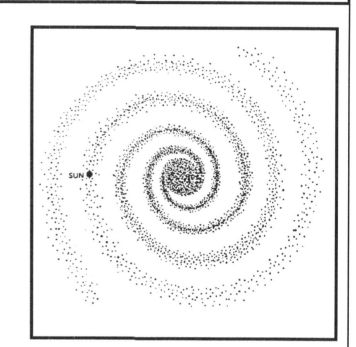

Page 61

	Hundred Billions	Ten Billions	Billions	Hundred Millions	Ten Millions	Millions	Hundred Thousands	Ten Thousands	Thousands	Hundreds	Tens	Ones
A.				2	2	5	0	0	0	0	0	0
B.				7	0	0	4	5	2	6	5	4
							6	4	3	4	1	1
						3	1	9	8	7	6	2
C.	9	9	9	9	9	9	9	9	9	9	9	9
		6	3	4	1	1	2	7	0	8	9	9
			1	9	8	8	4	6	5	4	3	2

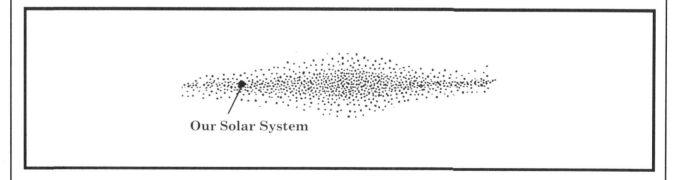

Our Solar System

Page 61 continued

	Hundred Billions	Ten Billions	Billions	Hundred Millions	Ten Millions	Millions	Hundred Thousands	Ten Thousands	Thousands	Hundreds	Tens	Ones
D.								3	3	0	0	0
				2	2	1	0	0	0	0	0	0
E.				1	0	0	0	0	0	0	0	0

A. two hundred twenty-five million

B. seven hundred million, four hundred fifty-two thousand, six hundred fifty-four

six hundred forty-three thousand, four hundred eleven

three million, one hundred ninety-eight thousand, seven hundred sixty-two

C. nine hundred ninety-nine billion, nine hundred ninety-nine million, nine hundred ninety-nine thousand, nine hundred ninety-nine

sixty-three billion, four hundred eleven million, four hundred sixty-five thousand, eight hundred ninety-nine

one billion, nine hundred eighty-eight million, four hundred sixty-five thousand four hundred thirty-two

D. thirty-three thousand

two hundred twenty-one million

E. one hundred million

Page 63 (1) The millions' places have seven, eight, and nine digits.
(2) The billions' places have ten, eleven, and twelve digits.
(3) 6 million million miles (9.5 million million km).
One hundred eighty-six thousand miles per second or 186,000.

Answer Key

Page 63 continued

    (4)   one complete year

    (5)   two hundred twenty-five billion years

    (6)   561,326,003
            654,305
                783
          64,860,995
             66,321
       693,285,655
                 25
              1,864
         2,671,884

Page 61 (2) cares
                     not another
                     earth

            (3) Teacher, check.

Page 65 Teacher, check.

Notes

United States Conversion Chart

Length

12 inches = 1 foot
36 inches = 1 yard
3 feet = 1 yard
5,280 feet = 1 mile
1,760 yard = 1 mile

Capacity

4 cups (c.) = 1 quart (qt.)
2 cups = 1 pint (pt.)
2 pints = 1 quart
8 pints = 1 gallon (gal.)
4 quarts = 1 gallon
3 teaspoons (tsp.) = 1 tablespoon
(Tbls.)

8 fluid (fl.) ounces (oz.) = 1 cup
16 fluid ounces = 1 pint
32 fluid ounces = 1 quart
128 fluid ounces = 1 gallon
8 quarts = 1 peck (pk)
4 pecks = 1 bushel (bu)

Time

60 second = 1 minute
60 minutes = 1 hour
24 hours = 1 day
7 days = 1 week
365 days = 1 year
12 months = 1 year
4 weeks = 1 months

Units

1 dozen = 12 units or items

Weight

16 ounces (oz.) = 1 pound (lb.)
2,000 pounds = 1 ton

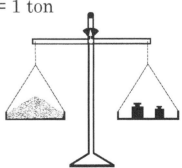

Metric Conversion Chart

Length and Distance

1 inch = 25 millimeters
1 inch = 2.5 centimeters
1 foot = .3 meters
1 foot = 30 centimeters
1 yard = .9 meters
1 mile = 1.6 kilometers

Volume and Capacity (liquid)

1 fluid ounce = 30 milliliters
1 pint (U.S.) = .47 liters
1 quart (U.S.) = .95 liters
1 gallon (U.S.) = 3.8 liters

Surface or Area

1 acre = .4 hectares

Weight and Mass

1 ounce = 28 grams
1 pound = .45 kilograms
1 ton = .9 metric tons

Temperature

$F° - 32 (5/9) = C°$

$C° \times (9/5) + 32 = F°$

Gardening Sheet

Lesson ___Two___ Subject ___Mathematics___

Title ___"A Place"___

In Season	Out of Season

(This is for In Season and Out of Season.)

In sketching your garden on paper, rule off rectangular shapes allowing 1/2 inch (12.5 millimeters) for each foot (30 centimeters) of the actual dimension of your plot. Then, take the list of vegetables you intend to grow and fit them into the space, row by row. Finding a <u>place</u> for each just as God has a <u>place</u> for you.

If possible run rows north and south to give them the most sun.

One purpose of planning on paper before planting is to keep most of the ground producing throughout the growing season. God wants you to produce the fruits of righteousness in your <u>place</u>.

A well-planned garden can combine small fruit trees with vegetable rows. The trees are widely separated so that the shade they cast does not retard vegetable production. Neatly planted rows are spaced 18 to 20 inches (45 to 50 centimeters) apart for cultivation.

If you plan to stake tomatoes, provide space for setting plants eight inches (20 centimeters) from poles. Use six-foot (180 centimeters) poles and space three feet (90 centimeters) apart.

If you grow a variety of vegetables and get average yields, 1,400 to 1,600 square feet (126 m^2-144 m^2) will produce enough for fresh use, for sharing, and for preserving for one person for one year. So a garden 75 x 100 feet (2250 cm. x 3,000 cm.) will feed a family of four to five. A garden of 24 x 50 feet or 30 x 50 feet (720 cm. x 1500 cm. or 900 cm. x 1500 cm.) would supply the summer and fall needs of a family of four and still have some to share and preserve. See the chart.

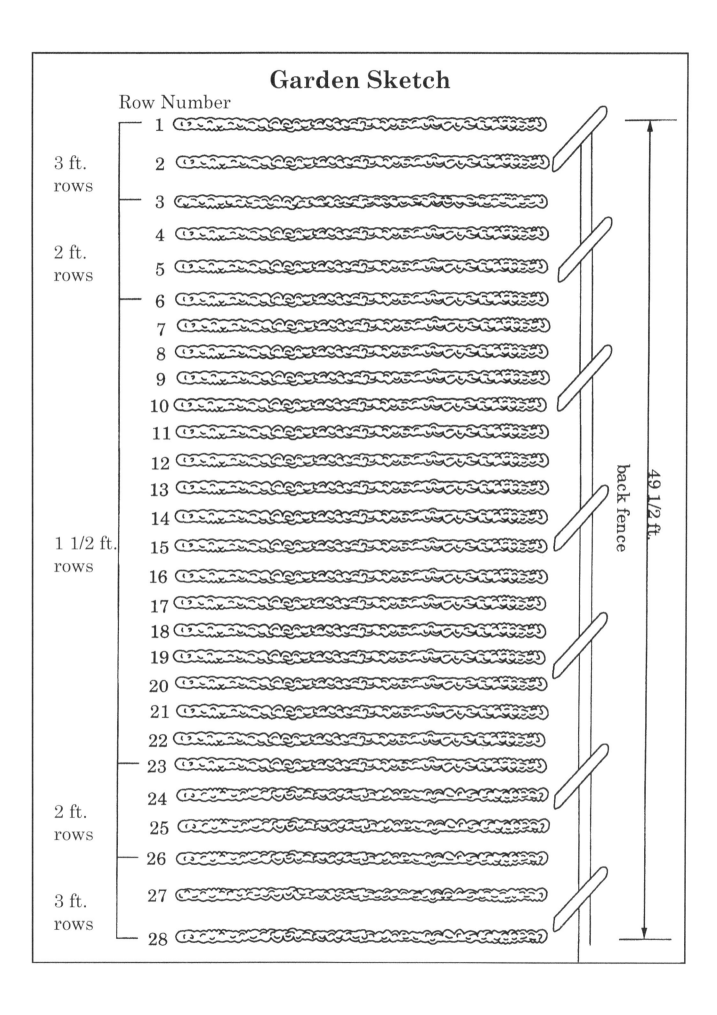

Student
Section

"Let not your heart be troubled:
ye believe in God, believe also in me.

In my Father's house are many mansions:
if it were not so, I would have told you.
I go to prepare a place for you.

And if I go and prepare a place for you,
I will come again, and receive you unto myself;
that where I am, there ye may be also."
John 14:1-3

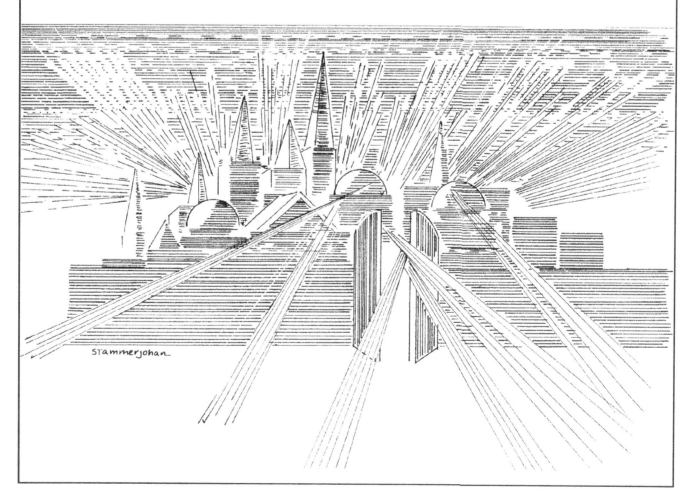

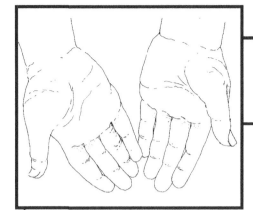

A Place

Home

Research
Place Value—Ones and Tens

"Even unto them will I give in mine house and within my walls

a place [an open hand indicating power, means, direction]

and a name [position, appellation, honor, authority, and

character] better than of sons and of daughters...."

Isaiah 56:5

Placed

God planned for the children of Israel to walk in the ways of obedience. But, because of their un-faithfulness to be **diligent** in their lives where they were placed, His purposes were carried out only through continual trials and humiliation. Just before and during the days of Jesus the Roman government ruled Israel. This was one of Israel's tribulations.*

There were twelve sons of Israel. They had many hardships. Their children made up what is known as the Jewish nation. Each child of Israel had a place or position in that nation.

Reflect

"...Hearken [hear] diligently

unto the voice of the Lord thy God...."

Deuteronomy 28:1

*great trouble or misery; severe trial; affliction

On the previous page
find 6 words
that mean "trials."

"Position" is one synonym for the word <u>place</u>. Israel was given the position of being a light unto the world. They were to prepare the people of earth to be ready to receive Christ when He came the first time. Did they fill their <u>place</u>?

"How many men of great natural abilities and high scholarship have failed when placed in positions of responsibility, while those of feebler intellect, with less favorable surroundings, have been wonderfully successful. The secret was, the former trusted to themselves, while the latter united with Him who is wonderful in counsel and mighty in working to accomplish what He will."*

The Hebrews thought a man's ultimate earthly happiness depended upon having one or more sons through whom the family name and children continue on, he may fear that his name and inheritance would be lost in Israel. However, God promises those who remain faithful to Him something even more wonderful than the joy of having children, that is, a <u>place</u> and *"a new name"* (Revelation 2:17), and the assurance that his name will be inscribed in the Book of Life (Revelation 3:5). God is concerned only with character and **diligence** to His principles of life. It is written: "This is the pledge that God's people are to make in these last days. Their acceptance with God depends on a faithful fulfillment of the terms of their agreement with Him. God includes in His covenant all who will obey Him. To all who will do justice and judgment, keeping their hand from doing any evil, the promise is, *'Even unto them will I give in mine house within my walls a place and a name better than of sons and of daughters: I will give them an everlasting name, that shall not be cut off.'*"**

Reflect

"The Lord brought them [Israel] over the same ground of <u>trial</u> repeatedly to prove whether they had yet learned His dealings and repent of their sinful disobedience and rebellious murmurings...If they would not glorify God in their <u>trials</u> and <u>adversity</u>, in their travels through the wilderness to the Canaan in prospect, while God was continually giving them unmistakable evidence of His power and glory, and His care for them, they would not magnify His name and glorify Him when established in the land of Canaan, surrounded with blessings and prosperity."***

*Counsels on Health 367-368 **1 Bible Commentary 1103   ***2 Testimonies 107

Review
Ones and Tens
Place I

A digit is a number.

If a number has only one digit it is in the ones' <u>place</u>.

If a number has two digits it has a tens' <u>place</u> and a ones' <u>place</u>.

1

12

"All should learn to be faithful in the least as well as in the greatest duty. Their work cannot bear the inspection of God unless it is found to include a faithful, **diligent**, economical care for the little things."*

Illustration

Fill in blank with the correct answer.

Israel (Jacob) had _____ sons

God/Israel	Ten's Place	One's Place
One-digit numbers in Ones' <u>place</u> (1—God)		1
Two-digit numbers in Tens' <u>place</u> (12—tribes)	1	2

*4 Testimonies 572

A Place – Student – Page 3

Place I

1. How many digits do these numbers have?

1 ____   9 ____   49 ____   65 ____

5 ____   10 ____   30 ____   29 ____

4 ____   89 ____   12 ____   51 ____

2 ____   6 ____   19 ____   24 ____

3 ____   8 ____   70 ____   11 ____

2. How many sons did Israel (Jacob) have? _____

How many tens are there? ____

How many ones are there? ____

The digit 12 means ___ ten and ___ ones.

There were ___ tens and ___ ones in the

illustration on page 3.

___ means ___ tens and ___ ones.

Jacob
Had
Twelve Sons

Reflect

"As you daily exercise the forces within you,
the task will grow less difficult,
until it will become second nature for you
to do duty, to be careful and **diligent**."*

2 Testimonies 428

Diligent Worker

John Eliot, on the day of his death, in his eightieth year, was found teaching the alphabet to an Indian child at his bedside. "Why not rest from your labors?" asked a friend. "Because," said the venerable man, "I have prayed to God to make me useful in my sphere, and He has heard my prayer; for now that I can no longer preach, He leaves me strength enough to teach this poor child his alphabet.

Read this story.

Remarkable Facts

600,000

Place III
Do the following word problem.

+ Women and Children

According to Exodus 12:37, the number of the children of Israel that went out of Egypt was *"about 600,000 on foot that were men, beside children."* This would imply a population of over 2,000,000. This has been deemed incredible by objectors to the Bible—incredible that so vast a multitude should have sprung in so short a time from the 70 souls that went down to that land in the time of Joseph. But the following calculation shows that it is not so incredible as might at first appear.

If we allow 31 years for a generation, the 215 years of actual residence in Egypt will give us seven generations. If from the number 70 we deduct Jacob, his daughter and granddaughter, we have 67 souls. Now, let us suppose that each of those and their male descendants had an average four sons and four daughters at the age of thirty—Benjamin had ten sons at that age—and counting seven generations, each thirty-one years, the total number of souls at the exodus would be as follows: (See the next column.)

```
                              67
                            x 4
1st generation          _____
                            x 4
2nd generation          _____
                            x 4
3rd generation          _____
                            x 4
4th generation          _____
                            x 4
5th generation          _____
                            x 4
6th generation          _____
                            x 4
7th generation  _____ males

                _____ females

Total           _____
```

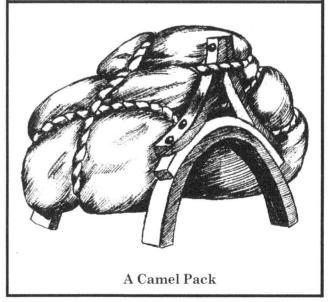

A Camel Pack

Research
A Special Place

"He came unto his own, and his own received him not."

John 1:11

Jesus came to His own people and they did not receive Him. They reverenced the temple more than God who gave it to them. *"But I say unto you, That in this place is one greater than the temple"* (Matthew 12:6).

"What Abraham was in the land of his sojourn, what Joseph was in Egypt, and Daniel in the courts of Babylon, the Hebrew people [Israel] were to be among the nations. They were to reveal God to men."* God wanted Israel to have a special place among the nations.

Reinforce
Serve

1. God has designed you to fill a special place in your family. Be **diligent** to serve your parents and brothers and sisters there.

2. Read the story, "**Diligent Workers.**"

The Desire of Ages 27

Illustration

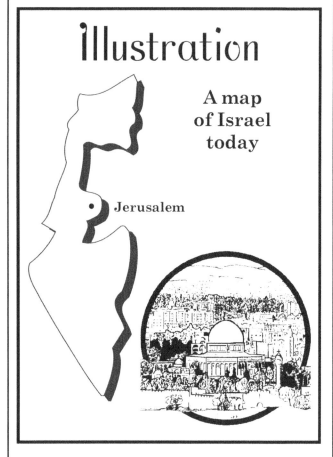

A map of Israel today

Jerusalem

Diligent Workers

Judson labored **diligently** for six years in Burma before he baptized a convert. At the end of these years he was asked what evidence he had of ultimate success. He replied, "As much as there is a God who will fulfill all His promises." From that small beginning there followed hundreds of churches and thousands of converts.

Mr. Benjamin, the United States Minister in Persia, many, many years ago, happened to remark to an artist he was employing at Teheran in doing some gilding, that he was giving more care than the money agreed upon would repay. He received the reply, "I do not work for money alone; I work because I love my profession."

Review
Place I

1. How many people are there in each picture?

1. Baby Jesus	2. Abraham, Joseph, Jacob	3. Israel's Sons

_____	_____	_____

"Ye shall diligently keep the commandments."

Deuteronomy 6:17

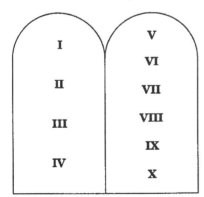

2. Fill in the first blank with the number of people in the pictures above, then print the name of the number in the second blank.

(1) ____ means one one _____ .

(2) ____ means three ones _____ .

(3) ____ means one ten and two ones.

_____

Research
Serving Self

The nation of Israel wanted to be important in this world. So, they served themselves instead of making Jesus most important in their lives and in the lives of others. Israel should have been true to God and practiced **diligence**. They should have kept His law and taken their place. Then they would have had honor and importance and a place above all the nations of the world. Instead they were subjects of the Roman government.

> "Thou hast commanded us to keep thy precepts diligently."
>
> Psalm 119:4

Read this story.

Others Not Self

Two boats were sent out from Dover to relieve a vessel in distress. The fury of the tempest overset one of them, which contained three sailors, one of whom sank. The two remaining sailors were floating on the deep; a rope was thrown to one of them from the other boat, but he refused it, crying out, "Fling it to Tom; he is just ready to go down. I can last some time longer." They did so; Tom was drawn into the boat. The rope was then flung to the selfless man, just in time to save him also from drowning.

Review – Place I – Fill in the numbers below.

1. World	2. Continents in the world	3. Law Promises
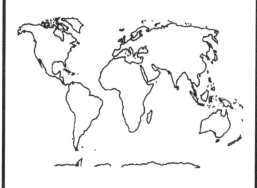		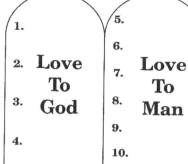

For "3. Law Promises":

1.
2. Love
3. To
4. God
5.
6.
7. Love
8. To
9. Man
10.

_____   _____   _____

1. _____ means one one.

   _____

2. _____ means seven ones.

   _____

3. _____ means one ten and zero ones.

   _____

Reflect

Israel Suffered Many Trials

Read Acts 14:22.

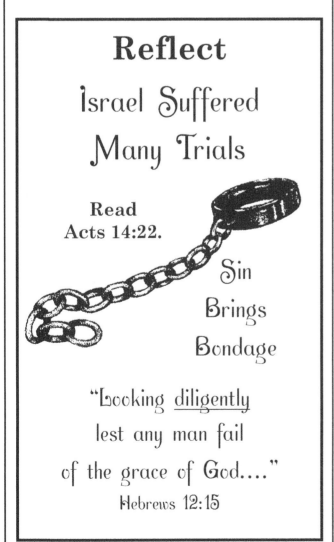

Sin

Brings

Bondage

"Looking <u>diligently</u> lest any man fail of the grace of God...."
Hebrews 12:15

Research
Trials

"Behold, I will gather them out of all countries, whither I have driven them in mine anger, and in my fury, and in great wrath; and I will bring them again unto this <u>place</u>, and I will cause them to dwell safely."
Jeremiah 32:37

Israel suffered many trials. They had to serve Babylon. Finally they came back from captivity to Jerusalem. We are told: *"Behold, I will gather them out of all countries, whither I have driven them in mine anger, and in my fury, and in great wrath; and I will bring them again unto this <u>place</u>, and I will cause them to dwell safely"* (Jeremiah 32:37).

They became careful about religious instruction. Synagogues (churches) were built. Schools were started. Soon however, these good churches and schools became corrupted. Heathen ideas and customs were brought into the churches and schools. Israel needed to give **diligence** to the things of God. God's ways needed to have a <u>place</u> in their lives instead of the heathen ways.

Review
Place I

Heathen Ideas and Customs Were Brought
Into the Churches and Schools.

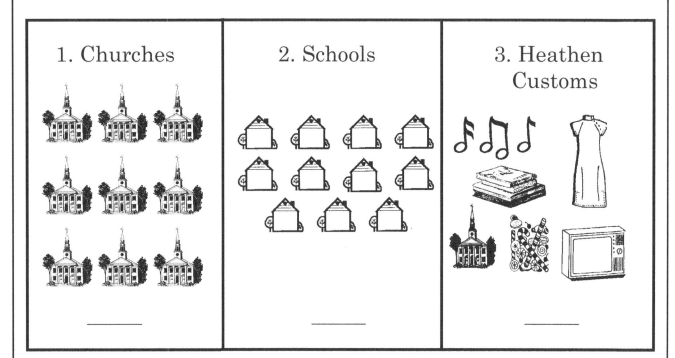

1. Churches	2. Schools	3. Heathen Customs
_____	_____	_____

Fill in the first blank with the number of pictures
in the above squares, then print the number
and the name of the number below.

1. _____ means nine ones. _____

2. _____ means eleven ones. _____

3. _____ means six ones. _____

Reflect

"When the Israelites first settled in Canaan they acknowledged the principles of the theocracy, and the nation prospered under the rule of Joshua. But increase of population and intercourse with other nations brought a change. The people adopted many of the customs of their heathen neighbors and thus sacrificed to a great degree their own peculiar, holy character. Gradually they lost their reverence for God and ceased to prize the honor of being His chosen people. Attracted by the pomp and display of heathen monarchs, they tired of their own simplicity...As they departed from obedience to God's law, they desired to be freed from the rule of their divine Sovereign; and thus the demand for a monarchy became widespread throughout Israel."

Patriarchs and Prophets 603

Research
Sacrifices and Ceremonies

Soon Israel became so busy with sacrifices and ceremonies. They lost the love of God. It had no <u>place</u> in their lives. In order to supply what they had lost they made more ceremonies. Israel became **diligent** in doing the many ceremonies. If only they had been **diligent** in loving and obeying God.

Loving and Obeying God

Reflect
Place I - II - III

Israel Became <u>Diligent</u> In Ceremonies. Are you <u>diligent</u> in loving and obeying God?

"It is when the vital principles of the kingdom of God are lost sight of, that ceremonies become <u>multitudinous</u> and <u>extravagant</u>. It is when the character building is neglected, when the adornment of the soul is lacking, when the simplicity of godliness is despised, that pride and love of display demand magnificent church edifices, splendid adornings, and imposing ceremonials."* **On a separate piece of paper define the underlined words.**

Review
Place I

1. Sacrifices	2. Ceremonies	3. Love and Obedience
	Ceremonies	
	Ceremonies	
	Ceremonies	
	Ceremonies	
	Ceremonies	
_____	_____	_____

Prophets and Kings 565

Fill in the first blank with the number of pictures on the previous page, then print the name of the number in the second blank.

1. _____ means eight ones. _____

2. _____ means five ones. _____

3. _____ means four ones. _____

"...Diligently learn the ways of my people."
Jeremiah 12:16

Research
Heavy Burdens

"For mine iniquities are gone over mine head: as an <u>heavy</u> <u>burden</u> they are too heavy for me."
Psalm 38:4

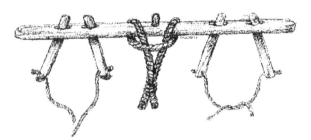

"...Many are called, but few are <u>chosen</u>...."
Matthew 22:14

The people of Israel became so weary under the heavy burden of all these sacrifices and ceremonies that they became discouraged. They did not understand God's character. He was calling them to *"Come unto me, all ye that labour and are heavy laden, and I will give you rest. Take my yoke upon you, and learn of me; for I am meek and lowly in heart: and ye shall find rest unto your souls. For my yoke is <u>easy</u>, and my <u>burden</u> is <u>light</u>"* (Matthew 11:28-30). God was saying, "I have a special <u>place</u> for you next to Me."

Israel desired the advent of the Messiah. But, they did not understand His mission nor recognize Him when He came. The people wanted to be delivered from the Romans. "They looked for the Messiah to come as a conqueror, to break the oppressor's [Roman] power, and exalt Israel to universal dominion. Thus the way was prepared for them to reject the Saviour."* God tells us: *"But seek ye first the kingdom of God, and his righteousness; and all these things shall be added unto you"* (Matthew 6:33).

*The Desire of Ages 30

God has a chosen people on earth today. It is important that they be **diligent** in their lives to serve God. If they are not, they will not be prepared, like Israel of old, for Christ's second coming.

"Let not your heart be troubled: ye believe in God, believe also in me. In my Father's house are many mansions: if it were not so, I would have told you. I go to prepare a place for you. And if I go and prepare a place for you, I will come again, and receive you unto myself; that where I am, there ye may be also" (John 14:1-3).

Review
Place I - II - III

1. What does **diligence** mean? ____

_____

_____

_____

2. Explain Israel's **diligence** (or lack of it). _____

_____

_____

_____

Remarkable Facts
Place III

• Did you ever calculate that the number of working hours in the mature part of life is only 135,000? Rest a moment on that thought. Between twenty-five years, which pass in the early part of life without much fruit, and the seventieth year of life, there are forty-five years of life which we call mature.

• Now, suppose that a man rests in every year fifty-two days for Sabbath, thirteen days for illness, vacation and other interruptions; and suppose that for forty-five consecutive years he works 300 days a year—a large average—that would give a man in the mature part of life, _____ days. Supposing that a man has health and industry enough to work ten hours in each of these 13,500 days, he will have _____ mature working hours. A man who is forty, however, has but _____ hours left; a man who is sixty has so few hours left that I do not want to shock you by mentioning their number.*

Fill in the missing blanks above.

Are you **diligent** in your daily tasks?

* Seed Corn for the Sower 415-416

Research
Waiting

"Study to show thyself
approved unto God,
a workman that needeth
not to be ashamed, rightly
dividing the word of truth."
II Timothy 2:15

"Only take heed to thyself,
and keep thy soul <u>diligently</u>,
lest thou forget the things
which thine eyes have seen,
and lest they depart from
thy heart all the days
of thy life: but teach them
thy sons, and thy sons' sons."
Deuteronomy 4:9

Israel had waited for more than a thousand years for the Messiah's coming. "In song and prophecy, in temple rite and household prayer" they told of His coming. "And yet at His coming they knew Him not." Why? Because of the misunderstanding they got in their education. It is written: *"Study to show thyself approved unto God, a workman that needeth not to be asham- ed, rightly dividing the word of truth"* (II Timothy 2:15).

It is important that we today, be **diligent** in studying His word, the Bible. We must pray for the Holy Spirit to help us understand correctly. Do you understand these words? *"Remember therefore from whence thou art fallen, and repent, and do the first works; or else I will come unto thee quickly, and will remove thy candlestick out of his <u>place</u>, except thou repent"* (Revela-

tion 2:5). The candlestick is the church and the light it gives to the world. The light comes from the Holy Spirit through the Holy Bible.

God has given us <u>sixty-six</u> books in the Bible. There are <u>thirty-nine</u> in the Old Testament and there are <u>twenty-seven</u> in the New testament. We need to **diligently** study them.

When spelling out two or more digit numbers such as 27, a hyphen (-) is always placed between the two words. (Example: Twenty-seven)

$$\begin{array}{r} 39 \text{ O.T.} \\ + 27 \text{ N.T.} \\ \hline 66 \text{ Books} \end{array}$$

Review
Place I

1. Books in the Bible	2. Books in Old Testament	3. Books in New Testament
	10 10 10 + 9	10 10 + 7
_____	_____	_____

Fill in the first blank with the number, then print the number name in the second blank.

1. _____ means six tens and six ones.

_____

2. _____ means three tens and nine ones.

_____

3. _____ means two tens and seven ones.

_____

4. The word **diligence** has _____ letters in it. _____ means nine ones. _____

The words <u>Holy</u> <u>Bible</u> have _____ letters in them. _____ means nine

ones. _____

     9 letters + 9 letters = 18 letters
                         or
     2 words x 9 letters = 18 letters

5. There are 18 letters in the words **diligence** and Holy Bible.

_____ means one ten and eight ones. _____

Read this story.

Watching

In Edinburgh, Scotland when the Queen first came, the vessel that brought her landed in the evening. The Lord Provost* concluded—"Oh, she will not come ashore till nine in the morning!" But what happened? The queen was very famous for taking people by surprise, and she landed between six and seven. The chief magistrate was sadly ashamed of himself. He did not lose his place; he was still what he was before; but he bitterly regretted that he had not been waiting to welcome her when she set foot upon the shore. I think that was the way it was when Jesus came the first time to this earth. Will it be that way with those who are not looking for Christ's second coming? They will regret not having waited for Him, when they might have been there to give Him a hearty welcome.

"Patience and **diligence**, like faith, remove mountains."
—William Penn

*the chief magistrate in a Scottish town

Research
Writing the Bible

"For the prophecy came not in old time by the will of man: but holy men of God spake as they were moved by the Holy Ghost."

ii Peter 1:21

About <u>forty</u> (40) **diligent** authors wrote the Bible.

Some <u>thirty</u> (30) authors wrote the books of the Old Testament.

The New Testament was written by about <u>eight</u> (8) men in about <u>fifty</u> (50) years.

The <u>thirty</u>-<u>nine</u> (39) Old Testament books were written in the Hebrew language, except for portions of Ezra and Daniel that were written in Aramaic.

The <u>twenty</u>-<u>seven</u> (27) New Testament books were written in Greek.

Review
Place I

1. Fill in the first blank with the number, and then write the number name in the second blank. Use the previous information.

_____ means 4 tens and 0 ones. _____

_____ means 3 tens and 0 ones. _____

_____ means 8 ones. _____

_____ means 5 tens and 0 ones. _____

_____ means 3 tens and 9 ones. _____

_____ means 2 tens and 7 ones. _____

Tens	Ones
4	0
3	0
0	8
5	0
3	9
2	7

40 is _____ tens and _____ ones. _____

30 is _____ tens and _____ ones. _____

8 is _____ ones. _____

50 is _____ tens and _____ ones._____

39 is _____ tens and _____ ones. _____

27 is _____ tens and _____ ones. _____

2. Read this story.

The Bible A Treasure

A young lady rejoicing in the freshness of the Savior's pardoning love, came to me one day bringing her little Bible. The book had been given her in early childhood by her dying mother, who had written these words on the fly-leaf:

"In this book a treasure lies,
    If you dig deep, you'll find the prize."

"O how often I have wondered what that meant," she said, "how often I have turned over these pages looking for the treasure, and now I have found it—yes, I have found it!" *The kingdom of heaven is like unto a treasure hid in a field; the which when a man hath found, he hideth, and for joy thereof goeth and selleth all that he hath, and buyeth that field."*
—*Seed Corn for the Sower*

Reflect
Bible Authorship
is Wonderful

The authorship of this book is wonderful. Here are words written by kings, by emperors, by princes, by poets, by sages, by philosophers, by fishermen, by statesmen; by men learned in the wisdom of Egypt, educated in the Schools of Babylon, trained at the feet of rabbis in Jerusalem. It was written by men in exile, in the desert, and in shepherds' tents, in *"green pastures"* and beside *"still waters."* Among its authors we find the fishermen, the tax-gatherer, the herdsman, the gatherer of sycamore fruit; we find poor men, rich men, statesmen, preachers, exiles, captains, legislators, judges—men of every grade and class. The authorship of this book is wonderful beyond all other books.

It required fifteen hundred years to write it, and the man who wrote the closing pages of it had no communication with the man who commenced it. How did these men, writing independently, produce such a book? Other books get out of date when they are ten or twenty years old; but this book lives on through the ages, and keeps abreast of the mightiest thought and intellect of every age.
—*H. L. Hastings*

Research
Work
"In all thy ways acknowledge him,
and he shall direct thy paths."
Proverbs 3:6

Are you **diligent** in the study of the Bible? Will you be prepared to take your place in God's plan for you? God has a place for you right now.

"The thoughts and ways of God in relation to His creatures are above our finite minds; but we may be assured that His children will be brought to fill the very place for which they are qualified, and will be enabled to accomplish the very work committed to their hands, if they will but submit their will to God, that His beneficent plans may not be frustrated by the perversity of man."* For we are promised: *"In all thy ways acknowledge him, and he shall direct thy paths"* (Proverbs 3:6).

"In the call of Abraham the Lord has said, *'I will bless thee... and thou shalt be a blessing:...and in thee shall all families of the earth be blessed'* (Genesis 12:2-3). The same teaching was repeated through the prophets. Even after Israel had been wasted by war and captivity, the promise was theirs,

'The remnant of Jacob shall be in the midst of many people as a dew from the Lord, as the showers upon the grass, that tarrieth not for man, nor waiteth for the sons of men' (Micah 5:7). Concerning the temple at Jerusalem, the Lord declared through Isaiah, *'Mine house shall be called a house of prayer for all people'* (Isaiah 56:7)."**

God was **diligent** in working with Israel so that they would be in the right place.

He is **diligent** in helping you fill your place.

Reinforce

Sing the Hymn,
"Anywhere With Jesus"

*Patriarchs and Prophets 638 **The Desire of Ages 27*

Reinforce

Planned

My God, I thank Thee, who has planned
A special life for me,
And <u>placed</u> me in this happy land
Where I hear about Thee.

Diligent Work

There comes over to our shores a poor stonecutter. The times are so bad at home that he is scarcely able to earn bread enough to eat; and by a whole year's stinting economy he manages to get together just enough to pay for a passage to this country. He comes, homeless and acquaintanceless, to New York, and wanders over to Brooklyn and seeks employment. He is ashamed to beg bread; and yet he is hungry. The yards are all full; but still, as he is an expert stonecutter, a man, out of charity, says, "Well, I will give you a little work—enough to enable you to pay for your board." And he shows him a block of stone to work on. What is it? One of many parts which are to form some ornament. Here is just a stem and a fern, and there is a petal of what is probably to be a flower. He goes to work on this stone, and most patiently shapes it. He carves that bit of a fern, putting all his skill and taste into it. And by-and-by the master says, *"Well done,"* and takes it away, and gives him another block, and tells him to work on that. He continues to work on the stone, from the rising of the sun till the going down of the same. And he only knows that he is earning his bread. He continues to put all his skill and taste into his work. He has no idea what use will be made of those few stems which he has been carving, until afterwards, when, one day, walking along the street, and looking up at the front of an art gallery, he sees the stones upon which he has worked. He did not know what they were for; but the architect did. As he stands looking at his work on that structure which is the beauty of the whole street, the tears drop down from his eyes, and he says, "I am glad I did it well." And every day, as he passes that way, he says to himself exultingly, "I did it well." He did not draw the design nor plan the building, and he knew nothing of what use was to be made of his work; but he took pains in cutting those stems. When he saw that they were a part of that magnificent structure, his soul rejoiced. Though the work which you are doing seems small, put your heart into it; do the best you can wherever you are; and by-and-by God will show you where He has put that work. And when you see it stand in that great structure which He is building you will rejoice in every single moment of fidelity with which you wrought. Do not let the seeming littleness of what you are doing now dampen your fidelity.

—*Adapted from Beecher*

> *"Whatsoever thy hand findeth to do, do it with thy might...."*
> **Ecclesiastes 9:10**

Review
Place I - II

To get from a lesser digit to a greater digit, you may increase or add by one (1).

Example:

0 - 1 - 2 - 3 - 4 - 5 - 6 - 7 - 8 - 9 - 10 - 11 - 12

---

1. Are the following numbers greater (G) or lesser (L) than seven (7)?
Write (L) or (G) beside each number.

2 _____   3 _____   1 _____

9 _____   6 _____   11 _____

12 _____   10 _____   5 _____

8 _____   4 _____   13 _____

2. Write out the numbers that remind you of Israel.

0 - <u>zero</u> _____

"All nations before him are as nothing; and they are counted to him less than nothing, and vanity."

Isaiah 40:17

Israel was <u>nothing</u> and God took them and made a great nation out of them. *"Ah Lord God! behold, thou hast made the heaven and the earth by thy great power and stretched out arm, and there is <u>nothing</u> too hard for thee"* (Jeremiah 32:17).

When Jesus came, the chosen people saw <u>nothing</u> attractive in His outward appearance. *"...And when we shall see him, there is no beauty that we should desire him"* (Isaiah 53:2).

Color the zero.

Print the name of the number in the blank provided.

1 - one _____

Jesus was to be the most important One in Israel. Even the devils acknowledged Him *"I know thee who thou art, the Holy One of God"* (Mark 1:24). But Israel did not recognize God's Son.

2 - two _____

God gave Israel the law to guide them. It has two parts as described in Matthew 22:37-40. *"Jesus said unto him, Thou shalt love the Lord thy God with all thy heart, and with all thy soul, and with all thy mind. This is the first and great commandment. And the second is like unto it, Thou shalt love thy neighbor as thyself. On these two commandments hang all the law and the prophets."*

"Thou hast commanded us to keep thy precepts **diligently.**"

Psalm 119:4

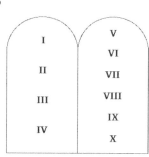

3 - three _____

Three men (Abraham, Joseph, and Daniel) gave examples to Israel as to where their place was to be among the nations. God tells us in Deuteronomy 17:6 that *"At the mouth of two witnesses, or three witnesses"* shall His word be established. Abraham, Joseph, and Daniel gave ample evidence to Israel. Read Matthew 18:16.

Color these numbers.

4 - four _____

When Jesus comes again He shall *"gather together his elect from the four winds, from one end of heaven to the other"* (Matthew 24:31). He will gather those that love and **diligently** obey Him.

5 - five _____

Israel had multiplied their ceremonies instead of cleansing their hearts and the result was: *"And five of them were wise, and five were foolish. They that were foolish took their lamps, and took no oil with them: But the wise took oil in their vessels with their lamps. While the bridegroom tarried, they all slumbered and slept"* (Matthew 25:2-5).

6 - six _____

Israel brought into the church and school the heathen customs as described in Proverbs 6:16-19. *"These six things doth the Lord hate: yea, seven are an abomination unto him: A proud look, a lying tongue, and hands that shed innocent blood, an heart that deviseth wicked imaginations, feet that be swift in running to mischief, A false witness that speaketh lies, and he that soweth discord among brethren."*

Color these numbers.

7 - seven _____

If only Israel would have kept the pure words of God as found in the Bible, they could have been an example to all the nations of the earth. *"The words of the Lord are pure words: as silver tried in a furnace of earth, purified <u>seven</u> times. Thou shalt keep them, O Lord, thou shalt preserve them from this generation for ever"* (Psalm 12:6-7).

8 - eight _____

Israel became busy with sacrifices rather than cleansing of heart. *"And on the sixth day <u>eight</u> bullocks, two rams, and fourteen lambs of the first year without blemish"* (Numbers 29:29).

9 - nine _____

Many synagogues (places of worship) were built after the captivity that Israel might receive proper instruction. However, pagan ideas came into the church. These ideas prevented many people from accepting Jesus as the Messiah. They rejected Him despite the wonderful miracles He performed while on earth. *"And Jesus answering said, Were there not ten cleansed? but where are the <u>nine</u>?"* (Luke 17:17).

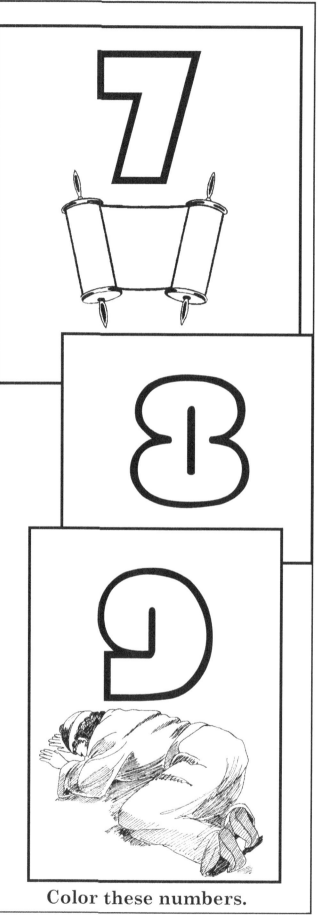

Color these numbers.

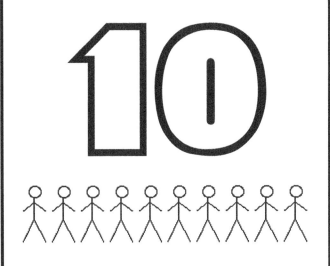

10 - ten _____

Keeping the <u>ten</u> commandment law correctly would have made Israel wise. Each day they could have grown stronger in the Lord as His word tells us in Ecclesiastes 7:19: *"Wisdom strengtheneth the wise more than <u>ten</u> mighty men which are in the city."* When the Messiah came, they, should have had the wisdom from above to recognized Him.

11 - eleven _____

Israel started schools after their captivity, but the pagan customs were soon being practiced in them. When we follow God's principles, the world will bow at our feet. Remember how Joseph's <u>eleven</u> brothers and all Egypt bowed before him. *"And he dreamed yet another dream, and told it his brethren, and said, Behold, I have dreamed a dream more; and, behold, the sun and the moon and the <u>eleven</u> stars made obeisance to me"* (Genesis 37:9).

12 - twelve _____

Israel is represented by the <u>twelve</u> sons of Jacob. *"All these are the <u>twelve</u> tribes of Israel: and this is it that their father spake unto them, and blessed them; every one according to his blessing he blessed them"* (Genesis 49:28).

Color these numbers.

Review
Place I

Tens	Ones

1. If a number has only one digit it is in what place? _____

2. If a number has two digits what places does it have? _____

3. In the space provided on the right, place the following numbers in the proper place.

    1, 2, 3, 4, 5, 6, 7, 8, 9, 10,
    11, 12, 27, 39, 66, 18, 40, 30, 50

4. Print the names of the following digits.

0_____

1_____

2_____

3_____

4_____

5_____

6_____

7_____

8_____

9_____

"And thou shalt teach them [Law] ***diligently*** *unto thy children..."*
Deuteronomy 6:7

10_____

11_____

12_____

5. How many ones and tens
are in each number?

35 has _____ tens and _____ ones.

22 has _____ tens and _____ ones.

11 has _____ tens and _____ ones.

46 has _____ tens and _____ ones.

53 has _____ tens and _____ ones.

66 has _____ tens and _____ ones.

91 has _____ tens and _____ ones.

75 has _____ tens and _____ ones.

64 has _____ tens and _____ ones.

6. Print the names of the following
digits.

39 _____

27 _____

66 _____

Reinforce

Work Should Begin Early

In the city of Basle, Switzerland, it was the custom to have all the clocks of the city set an hour ahead of time, for the following reason: Once an enemy was moving upon the city, and their stratagem was to take the city at twelve o'clock noon. The cathedral clock, by mistake, struck one instead of twelve; and so the enemy thought that they were too late to carry out the stratagem. They gave up the assault, and the city was saved; and it was arranged for many years that the clock struck one when it was twelve, and twelve when it was eleven.

O children of God, engage in Christian work—set your clocks on, if you want to save the city! Better get to your work too early than came too late. The King's business requires haste.

> "...She hath a place prepared of God...."
>
> Revelation 12:6

Remind

1. As a member of your family, you have a place to fill. It may be washing dishes, cleaning the living room, stacking wood, or making things easier for your parents in some other way. You may be the one who always sings and is cheering all the others. You are an important part of your earthly and heavenly family. Be **diligent**!

2. Israel had an appointed <u>place</u> to work in the past. What place has God given to you to work in today?

3. A **diligent** person will set a pace when working, then keep at it.

A gentleman was overlooking a man at work on his grounds who was emptying a tank by means of a bucket into the drain. "What a lazy fellow!" he thought. "I could fill that bucket twice to his once." The more he looked, the more his indignation increased, until at last he determined to show the man how to do his work. "Are you not ashamed," he asked, "to pour no more than two or three pails a minute!" The man smiled, but said he could not well do more. "Well, I'll show you that more can be done." So he went to work with great zeal, and poured out six or eight pails a minute. "Now," he said triumphantly, handing back the pail, "I've taught you a lesson. I hope you will profit by it." "Please your honor," said the man, "would you be kind enough to go on in that way another two minutes?" "Why?" "Because I never doubted but six pails could be poured in a minute; but what I want to know is, how long you could keep on at that rate."

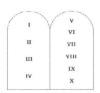

Research
Place Value—Hundreds

"Thy testimonies also are my delight, and my counselors."
Psalm 119:24

The Bible

God designed that each of His chosen people have a <u>place</u>! They were to keep (preserve) among men the knowledge of His law, and the symbols and prophecies that pointed to the Saviour. **Diligence** was to be their watchword. They could only do this as they understood and practiced God's law. The Bible is a book that explains how to keep the law of God.

God tells us: *"Thy testimonies also are my delight, and my <u>counselors</u>"* (Psalm 119:24).

There are nine hundred and twenty-nine (929) carefully <u>placed</u> chapters in the Old Testament.

There are two hundred and sixty (260) carefully <u>placed</u> chapters in the New Testament.

Reflect

"Even unto them will I give in mine house and within my walls <u>a place</u> and a name better than of sons and of daughters."
Isaiah 56:5

"The English Bible is a book which if everything else in our language should perish, would alone suffice to show the whole extent of its beauty and power."
—*Macaulay*

If a number has three digits, the third <u>place</u> is called the hundreds' <u>place</u>!

Chapters

929

260

Knowledge of the Bible

A little girl being asked by a priest to attend his religious instruction, refused, saying it was against her father's wishes.

The priest said she should obey him, not her father.

"Oh, sir, we are taught in the Bible, *'Honor thy father and thy mother.'*"

"You have no business to read the Bible," said the priest.

"But, sir, Our Saviour said, *"Search the Scriptures'* (John 5:39)."

"That was only to the Jews, and not to children, and you don't understand it," said the priest in reply.

"But Paul said to Timothy, *'From a child thou hast known the holy Scriptures'* (II Timothy 3:15)."

"Oh," said the priest, "Timothy was being trained to be a Bishop, and taught by the authorities of the church."

"Oh, no, sir," said the child; "he was taught by his mother and his grandmother."

On this the priest turned her away, saying she "knew enough of the Bible to poison a parish."

—*Seed Corn for the Sower*

The Bible Adapted to Our Daily Lives

There is no other book which associates itself in the same way and to the same extent with the joys and sorrows of human life, with births, marriages, and burials, with our journeys, our country walks, our conversation round the family hearth, our silence by the sick-bedside—no other which like this would bear to be read over the coffin of the dead, at the mouth of the sepulchre. Why is it that people in their troubles cleave to what is written here as they do to nothing else in this wide world? Says Horne, "the fairest flowers of human wit, after a few perusals, like gathered flowers, wither in our hands and lose their fragrancy; but these unfading plants of paradise [The Psalm] become, as we are more accustomed to them, more and more beautiful, their bloom appears to be daily heightened, fresh odors are emitted, and new sweets are extracted from them."

—*John Stoughton*

Review
Place I - II

	Hundreds	Tens	Ones
One digit numbers in ones' <u>place</u>			1
Two digit numbers in tens' <u>place</u>		1	0
Three digit numbers in hundreds' <u>place</u>	9	2	9

1. There are 929 chapters in the Old Testament._____ is in the hundreds' <u>place</u>.

There are _____ digits. 2 is in the _____ <u>place</u>. 9 is in the _____ <u>place</u>.

2. There are 260 chapters in the New Testament. 2 is in the _____ <u>place</u>.

_____ is in the tens' <u>place</u>. 0 is in the _____ <u>place</u>.

Reflect

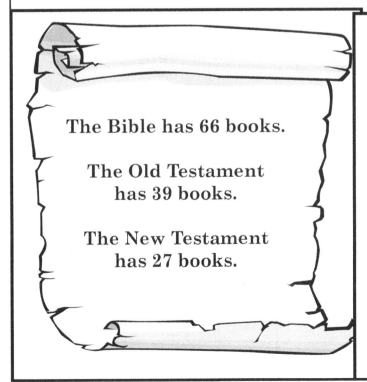

The Bible has 66 books.

The Old Testament has 39 books.

The New Testament has 27 books.

"For I testify unto every man that heareth the words of the prophecy of this book, If any man shall add unto these things, God shall add unto him the plagues that are written in this book:

"And if any man shall take away from the words of the book of this prophecy, God shall take away his part out of the book of life, and out of the holy city, and from the things which are written in this book."
Revelation 22:18-19

3. For the hundred's place there are always _____ digits.

4. For the tens' place there are always _____ digits.

5. For the ones' place there are always _____ digits.

6. How many chapters are there in the book of Psalms? _____

_____ is in the ones' place.

_____ is in the tens' place.

_____ is in the hundred's place.

7. There are how many chapters in Isaiah and Jeremiah? _____

_____ is in the ones' place.

_____ is in the tens' place.

_____ is in the hundred's place.

Diligence

"And whatsoever ye do,
do it heartily, as to the Lord,
and not unto men."
Colossians 3:23

Words in

1st Commandment =   8

2nd Commandment = 91

3rd Commandment = 27

4th Commandment = 94

God's Law

5th Commandment = 22

6th Commandment =   4

7th Commandment =   5

8th Commandment =   4

9th Commandment =   9

10th Commandment = 33

Love to God = 220 words
Love to Man = 77 words
Whole Law = 297 words

Fill in the following chart using the previous information.

Commandment	Hundreds	Tens	Ones	Hundreds	Tens	Ones	Commandment
1			___		___	___	5
2		___	___			___	6
3		___	___			___	7
4		___	___			___	8
						___	9
					___	___	10
Total	___	___	___		___	___	Total

"...God has called us to serve Him in the temporal affairs of life. Diligence in this work is as much a part of true religion as is devotion."
Christ's Object Lessons 343

Reflect

The Law

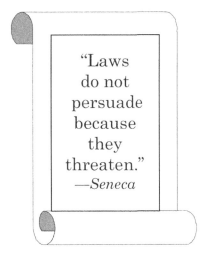

"Laws do not persuade because they threaten."
—*Seneca*

An Oriental custom tells that when a debt had to be settled, either by payment or forgiveness, it was the usage for the creditor to take the cancelled bond and nail it over the door of him who had owed it, that all passers-by might see that it was paid. Oh blessed story of our remission! There is the cross, the door of grace, behind which a bankrupt world lies in hopeless debt to the law. See Jesus, our bondsman and brother, coming forth with the long list of our indebtedness in His hand. He lifts it up where God and angels and men may see it, and then, as the nail goes through His hand, it goes through the bond of our transgressions to cancel it for ever. [This is what He does for His people.]
—*Clerical Library*

The wife of a drunkard once found her husband in a filthy condition with torn clothes, matted hair, bruised face, asleep in the kitchen, having come home from a drunken revel. She sent for a photographer, and had a portrait of him taken in all his wretched appearance, and placed it on the mantel beside another portrait taken at the time of his marriage, which showed him handsome and well dressed, as he had been in other days. When he became sober he saw the two pictures, and awakened to a consciousness of his condition, from which he arose to a better life. Now, the office of the law is not to save men, but to show them their true state as compared with the Divine standard. It is like a glass, in which one seeth *"what manner of man he is."*

The strength of a chain is only equal to its weakest part. Snap one link, and what avails the strength of all the rest until that broken or loose link be welded again? *"Whosoever shall keep the whole law, and yet offend in one, he is guilty of all."* The question of small sins is as clear as a problem of Euclid*—a question of a drop of prussic acid and a vial full or a sea full.
—*Grosart*

*A Greek mathematician; geometry

Man's "Laws are like spiders' webs: if some light or powerless thing falls into them, it is caught, but a bigger one can break through and get away."
—*Solon*

"Laws too gentle are seldom obeyed; too severe, seldom executed."
—*Benjamin Franklin*

Total of all words in the Law of God

Hundreds   Tens   Ones

____   ____   ____

Research
The Right Place

Numbers have <u>place</u> value, and they are valuable when they are in the right <u>place</u>. If they are not in the right <u>place</u> they are like: *"...a man that wandereth from his <u>place</u>"* (Proverbs 27:8).

Did Israel ever take the <u>place</u> God graciously gave them? No!

We can be **diligent** students of the Word of God. We can learn which <u>place</u> God has for us and **diligently** occupy that <u>place</u>. *"Lord, thou hast been our dwelling <u>place</u> in all generations"* (Psalm 90:1). Ask God to help you stay in the <u>right place</u>.

The Jews lost their <u>place</u> in God's plan.

Reinforce
Right Place At the Right Time

A lady, walking out one day near a river, saw a man with his coat and hat off, and she thought directly he meant to drown himself. She prayed that the Lord would give her some words to stop him. Accordingly, she walked on until she came up to him, when he turned and said, "A beautiful river, Ma'am," "Yes," she replied; "but there is another river—a river that makes glad the people of God. Do you know that river?" "No, Ma'am," he said. She tried to speak more, but her tongue was tied, and she left him without another word. She went home to her husband, and told him what she thought, and he sent off some men at once to see if he was still there. No, he was gone; but the coat and hat were in the same place. They dragged the river, but no traces of him could be found. They asked at the police station about him, but no one knew what was become of him. Twenty years after that this lady was in a chapel, and saw a man looking very earnestly at her. She thought, "I know that face; where have I seen him?" While she was trying to remember he leaned over her shoulder and said, "There is another river. Do you know that river?" She immediately remembered he was the man to whom she said those words twenty years ago. He told her he was going to drown himself, and her words deterred him from it. He had fled to Jesus, and found peace through believing. *—H. L. Hastings*

"For yet a little while, and the wicked shall not be: yea, thou shalt **diligently** consider his <u>place</u>, and it shall not be."
Psalm 37:10

1 – 10   Review – 100
Place I - II

Place Value
<u>Place</u> <u>value</u> tells whether a digit is in the ones', tens', or hundreds' place.

Digital Value
<u>Digital</u> <u>value</u> tells how many ones, how many tens,
and how many hundreds there are.

Example – 929

What is the <u>place</u> <u>value</u> of the first 9? Hundreds' place.

What is the <u>digital</u> <u>value</u> of the first 9? Nine hundred.

929 means 900 + 20 + 9, which is, 9 hundreds, 2 tens, and 9 ones.

---

1. Every number has two values, ___ ___ ___ ___ ___ value and

___ ___ ___ ___ ___ ___ ___ value.

2. What does place value tell you? _____

Read this story.

In the Right Place to Hear the Word

There was a man while we were in London, who got out a little paper called "The Moody and Sankey Humbug." He used to have it to sell to the people coming into the meeting. After he had sold a great many thousand copies of that number he wanted to get out another number; so he came into the meeting to get something to put into the paper. The power of the Lord was present, and the arrow of conviction went down deep into his heart. He went out, not to write a paper, but to destroy his paper that he had written, and so tell what the Holy Ghost had done for him. —*Moody*

3. What does digital value tell you? _____

4. Following the example, break down these numbers in the right column.

Example:		
2 hundreds	6 tens	0 ones

____ hundreds ____ tens ____ ones

____ hundreds ____ tens ____ ones

____ hundreds ____ tens ____ ones

____ hundreds ____ tens ____ ones

____ hundreds ____ tens ____ ones

____ hundreds ____ tens ____ ones

Remarkable Facts About the Bible:

- 260 chapters in the New Testament

- 220 words in the first four commandments

- 77 words in the last six commandments

- 297 words in the Ten Commandment Law

- Psalm 119 is the longest chapter

- 176 verses are in the longest chapter

- Psalm 117 is the shortest chapter

- 600 verses of Mark appear in Matthew

- 406 estimated references to "blood"

- 404 verses in Revelation

- Psalm 103 is one of the most exalted descriptions of the character of God.

_____ hundreds _____ tens _____ ones

_____ hundreds _____ tens _____ ones

_____ hundreds _____ tens _____ ones

_____ hundreds _____ tens _____ ones

Reinforce

1. If asked by father to weed a portion of the garden, be in that <u>place</u> and not in another. This is where your heavenly Father would want you to be! God says: *"Be thou **diligent** to know the state of thy flocks, and look well to thy herds"* (Proverbs 27:23). Explain this verse to your teacher.

2. Find spiritual lessons in the work you have been assigned to do. Meditate on these lessons while you **diligently** fulfill your task.

Work Can Be Fun!

Wishing one day to be rid of the loose stones upon my lawn, I thought myself very clever when I had erected a target just over the border, and asked certain boys to throw stones at it from my place for a prize. But it suddenly occurred to the eager young men that it was work they were doing for me, and all the fun gave way to utter disgust! Now, the deep-seated hatred that some children and older folks have for work is because they have not learned to love it. In the beginning before sin, God created man to enjoy his work! Sin has brought the curse of seeing it as drudgery.

—*Adapted from W. M. Baker*

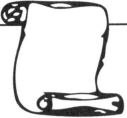

Review

Place I – II

1. What is the third place called?_____

How many digits does it have? _____

2. Place the following numbers in the chart. Think of them as words in the Bible.

| 742 | 772 | 166 | 789 | 487 | 269 | 347 | 666 |

| 576 | 372 | 292 | 777 |

Circle all the sevens in the above numbers. Tell what place each seven is in by writing it below.

___ ___   ___ ___   ___ ___   ___ ___

___ ___   ___ ___   ___ ___

___ ___   ___ ___   ___ ___

Hundreds	Tens	Ones
___	___	___
___	___	___
___	___	___
___	___	___
___	___	___
___	___	___
___	___	___
___	___	___
___	___	___
___	___	___
___	___	___

Color the words to this verse and read them.

"Thy word is very pure: therefore thy servant loveth it."
Psalm 119:140

3. Every number has _____ values.

Name them. _____ value, and

_____ value.

4. Write the names of the twelve digits.

_____

_____

_____

_____

_____

_____

_____

_____

_____

10 11
12

Reflect

"In tilling the soil, in discipling and subduing the land, lessons may constantly be learned. No one would think of settling upon a raw piece of land, expecting it at once to yield a harvest. Earnestness, **diligence**, and persevering labor are to be put forth in treating the soil preparatory to sowing the seed. So it is in the spiritual work in the human heart. Those who would be benefited by the tilling of the soil must go forth with the word of God in their hearts. They will then find the fallow ground of the heart broken by the softening, subduing influence of the Holy Spirit. Unless hard work is bestowed on the soil, it will not yield a harvest. So with the soil of the heart: the Spirit of God must work upon it to refine and discipline it before it can bring forth fruit to the glory of God."
—*Christ's Object Lesson* 88

Reinforce
Place I
Color these numbers.

1 2 3
4 5 6
7 8 9

Research
Place Value—Thousands, Ten Thousands, Hundred Thousands

Chosen

"...But I have <u>chosen</u> you out of the world,

therefore the world hateth you."

John 15:19

What does it mean to be <u>chosen</u>? It means to be selected or marked for favor or special privileges. When God <u>chooses</u> a people it means He calls and they respond. *"...But I have <u>chosen</u> you out of the world, therefore the world hateth you"* (John 15:19).

As we look out into the vast universe and observe the multitude of inhabited worlds without number we exclaim, *"What is man, that thou art mindful of him? and the son of man, that thou visiteth him? For thou hast made him a little lower than the angels, and hast crowned him with glory and honor. Thou madest him to have dominion over the works of thy hands; thou hast put all things under his feet"* (Psalm 8: 4-6).

Reflect

It is a remarkable fact, that while the baser metals are diffused through the body of the rocks, gold and silver usually lie in veins; collected together in distinct metallic masses. They are in the rocks but not of them...And as by some power in nature God has separated them from the base and common earths, even so by the power of His grace will He separate His chosen from a reprobate and rejected world. *—Guthrie*

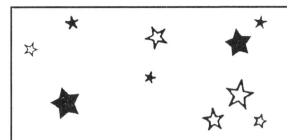

From our little world in the vast Milky Way galaxy spread other galaxies without number. Yet, the great God of the universe <u>chose</u> Israel of old to prepare the way of His Son. In like manner He has <u>chosen</u> you to prepare the way for His second coming. Are you responding? Are you being **diligent** in your <u>place</u>? Or like Israel of old, are you caught up in churches, schools, sacrifices, and ceremonies? Hopefully you are one of the number described in I Peter 2:9. *"But ye are a <u>chosen</u> generation, a royal priesthood, an holy nation, a peculiar people; that ye should show forth the praises of him who hath called you out of darkness into his marvellous light."*

The Milky Way is three thousand (3,000) parsecs* in thickness and thirty thousand (30,000) in diameter. There are approximately one hundred billion (100,000,000,000) stars in it. It reminds me of the text: *"As the host of heaven cannot be numbered, neither the sand of the sea measured: so will I multiply the seed of David my servant, and the Levites that minister unto me"* (Jeremiah 33:22). ***A unit of distance used in computing the distances of stars.**

Choice

Over the unrecorded death and grave of one of Franklin's arctic explorers, found on the ice-bound shore of Beechy Island, were found these words: *"<u>Choose</u> you this day whom you will serve."* It told of one, who, in the Polar zone of death and night, had found the answer to an eternal summer someday in the paradise of God. Looking over an endless sea of ice, the dying man saw that his eternity would be according to the <u>choice</u> which he had made. There can be no intermediate <u>choice</u>; for if one neither loves nor hates the service of his Creator, he has never <u>chosen</u> Him, and there should be no halting between two opinions.
—*Adapted From John Waugh*

"Blessed is the man whom thou <u>choosest</u>, and causest to approach unto thee, that he may dwell in thy courts..."
Psalm 65:4

Review
Place II - III
(Include Place I child if he can do these problems.)

If a number has four digits, it is in the thousands' <u>place</u>.

If a number has five digits, it is in the ten thousands' <u>place</u>.

If a number has six digits, it is in the hundred thousands' <u>place</u>.

1 Parsec = 3.26 light years (or about 19.2 trillion miles).

"As a man thinketh so is he, and as a man <u>chooseth</u> so is he."
—Emerson

1. Fill in the chart below.

Milky Way Galaxy				
	ten thousands	thousands	hundreds	tens	ones
thickness		—	—	—	—
diameter	—	—	—	—	—

Write the number 3,000:
_____ _____

Write the number 30,000:
_____ _____

Research
Set Apart

"...Look now toward heaven, and tell [Count] the stars, if thou be able to number them...."

Genesis 15:5

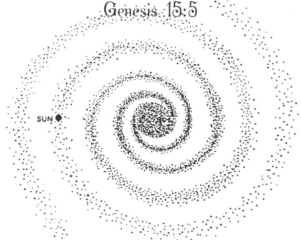

God has <u>chosen</u> you out of the Milky Way galaxy, and all other galaxies without number, to be His child. Will you **diligently** seek to serve Him where He has <u>placed</u> you?

Where do you live? That is where you need to serve God. *"...Tell [Count] the stars, if thou be able to number them..."* (Genesis 15:5).

The following chart lists 16 galaxies including the Milky Way with their size and distance from the Earth.

Reflect

Every Little Light

Every little star
Every little light
From its <u>place</u> afar
Helps to spread the light.

Diligently Work

"The work of many may appear to be restricted by circumstances; but, wherever it is, if performed with faith and **diligence** it will be felt to the uttermost parts of the earth. Christ's work when upon earth appeared to be confined to a narrow field, but multitudes from all lands heard His message. God often uses the simplest means to accomplish the greatest results."

The Desire of Ages 822

There are one to four trillion stars in each galaxy.

Shape	Galaxy	Distance	Diameter
Spiral	Milky Way		30,000
Irregular	Large Magellanic	48,000	10,000
Irregular	Small Magellanic	56,000	8,000
	Ursa Minor	70,000	1,000
Elliptical	Sculptor	83,000	2,200
	Draco	100,000	1,400
	Fornax	190,000	6,600
	Leo II	230,000	1,600
	Leo I	280,000	1,500
	NGC 6822	460,000	2,700
	NGC 147	570,000	3,000
	NGC 185	570,000	2,300
	NGC 205	680,000	5,000
	NGC 221	680,000	2,400
	IC 1613	680,000	5,000
Normal	Andromeda	680,000	40,000
Spiral	NGC	720,000	17,000

Irregular Galaxy

**Notice that a comma is placed after each three numbers.
This makes it easier for you to read the numbers
and keep numbers in columns.**

Review

Place II - III

(Include Place I child if he can do these problems.)

1. Using the grid on the following pages, <u>place</u> the appropriate number adding commas where needed. Then write this number out.

Galaxy	distance /diameter	hundred thousands	ten thousands	one thousands	hundreds	tens	ones
Milky Way	distance						
"	diameter		3	0	0	0	0
Large Mag	distance		—	—	—	—	—
"	diameter		—	—	—	—	—
Small Mag	distance		—	—	—	—	—
"	diameter		—	—	—	—	—
Ursa Minor	distance		—	—	—	—	—
"	diameter		—	—	—	—	—
Sculptor	distance		—	—	—	—	—
"	diameter		—	—	—	—	—
Draco	distance	—	—	—	—	—	—
"	diameter			—	—	—	—
Fornax	distance	—	—	—	—	—	—
"	diameter			—	—	—	—
Leo II	distance	—	—	—	—	—	—
"	diameter			—	—	—	—

Diligent (adjective) • **Diligence** (noun) • **Diligently** (adverb)

Galaxy	distance /diameter	hundred thousands	ten thousands	one thousands	hundreds	tens	ones
Leo I	distance	___	___	___	___	___	___
"	diameter			___	___	___	___
NGC6822	distance	___	___	___	___	___	___
"	diameter			___	___	___	___
NGC147	distance	___	___	___	___	___	___
"	diameter			___	___	___	___
NGC185	distance	___	___	___	___	___	___
"	diameter			___	___	___	___
NGC205	distance	___	___	___	___	___	___
"	diameter			___	___	___	___
NGC221	distance	___	___	___	___	___	___
"	diameter			___	___	___	___
IC1613	distance	___	___	___	___	___	___
"	diameter			___	___	___	___
Andromeda	distance	___	___	___	___	___	___
"	diameter		___	___	___	___	___
NGC	distance	___	___	___	___	___	___
"	diameter		___	___	___	___	___

"Vigilance and fidelity have been required of Christ's followers in every age; but now that we are standing upon the very verge of the eternal world, holding the truths we do, having so great light, so important a work, we must double our **diligence**."

5 Testimonies 460-461

Galaxy	distance /diameter	Write out the appropriate number, placing commas where needed.
Milky Way	distance	_____
"	diameter	_____
Large Mag	distance	_____
"	diameter	_____
Small Mag	distance	_____
"	diameter	_____
Ursa Minor	distance	_____
"	diameter	_____
Sculptor	distance	_____
"	diameter	_____
Draco	distance	_____
"	diameter	_____
Fornax	distance	_____
"	diameter	_____
Leo II	distance	_____
"	diameter	_____
Leo I	distance	_____
"	diameter	_____
NGC6822	distance	_____
"	diameter	_____

Diligence is a word which also means a fast public stagecoach, which was formerly used in France and other parts of Europe.

Galaxy	distance /diameter	Write out the appropriate number, placing commas where needed.
NGC147	distance	_____
"	diameter	_____
NGC185	distance	_____
"	diameter	_____
NGC205	distance	_____
"	diameter	_____
NGC221	distance	_____
"	diameter	_____
IC1613	distance	_____
"	diameter	_____
Andromeda	distance	_____
"	diameter	_____
NGC	distance	_____
"	diameter	_____

Reinforce

Sing this hymn.

Watch, Ye Saints

"Watch, ye saints, with eyelids waking;
Lo! the powers of heaven are shaking;
Keep your lamps all trimmed and burning,
Ready for your Lord's returning."

"Lo, He comes, Lo! Jesus comes;
Lo! He comes, He comes all glorious!
Jesus comes to reign victorious,
Lo! He comes, yes, Jesus comes."

Remind

If only Israel had been true to God, He could have accomplished His purposes through them. Today He has <u>chosen</u> you to be His child to accomplish His purposes. Like the billions of stars in each galaxy, you too, can **diligently** shine for Him in this world saying: *"Behold, He cometh...."*

Review

Place II - III
(Include Place I if the child can do these problems.)

Remember, each digit in a number has a place value and a digital value. In the number 7,777 the place value and digital values are:

1. Place (How Many)

Thousands	Hundreds	Tens	Ones
7	7	7	7

2. Digital (Value)

Seven Thousand	7,000
Seven Hundred	700
Seventy	70
Seven	7
	7,777

Reflect

Seven in the Bible is a perfect number. God has a perfect number of stars in His universe.

"The heavens call to you, and circle around you, displaying to you their eternal splendors, and your eye gazes only to earth."
—Dante

"The heavens declare the glory of God; and the firmament sheweth his handiwork."

Psalm 19:1

Place Value
The place value of the first seven is the ones' place.
The place value of the second seven is the tens' place.
The place value of the third seven is the hundreds' place.
The place value of the fourth seven is the thousands' place.

Digital Value
The digital value of the first digit is seven.
The digital value of the second digit is seventy times greater.
The digital value of the third digit is seven hundred times greater.
The digital value of the fourth digit is seven thousand times greater.

**It is important to be in the right <u>place</u>,
and to know the proper value of that <u>place.</u>**

Research
Valuable

"I will make a man more precious than fine gold;

even a man than the golden wedge of Ophir."

Isaiah 13:12

" *'The Spirit of the Lord God is upon me; because the Lord hath anointed me to preach good tidings unto the meek, He hath sent me to bind up the brokenhearted, to proclaim liberty to the captives, and the opening of the prison to them that are bound.'* He is the only One that has power to do it. Here the great price has been paid for souls sunk in sin. Man must be of <u>value</u>. Christ weighs him. Christ's taking human nature upon Himself shows that He places a <u>value</u> upon every soul. *'What? know ye not that your body is the temple of the Holy Ghost which is in you, which ye have of God, and ye are not your own? For ye are bought with a price: therefore glorify God in your body, and in your spirit, which are God's.'* This is the <u>value</u> God places upon man, and again He says, *'I will make a man more precious than fine gold; even a man than the golden wedge of Ophir.'* But God will do nothing without the co-operation of the human agent."*

*Temperance 287

Reflect
Gold
of Ophir

Christ Places
A High Value On Every Soul

"In the estimation of God, a pure heart is more precious than the gold of Ophir. A pure heart is the temple where God dwells, the sanctuary where Christ takes up His abode. A pure heart is above everything that is cheap or low; it is a shining light, a treasure house from which come uplifting, sanctified words. It is a place where the imagery of God is recognized, and where the highest delight is to behold His image. It is a heart that finds its whole and only pleasure and satisfaction in God, and whose thoughts and intents and purposes are alive with godliness. Such a heart is a sacred place; it is a treasury of all virtue...."

—*My Life Today* 263

Remind

Each day as you are <u>chosen</u> to do certain chores, like vacuuming, raking, feeding animals, do your work with **diligence**.

"...Let it be **diligently** done...."
Ezra 7:23

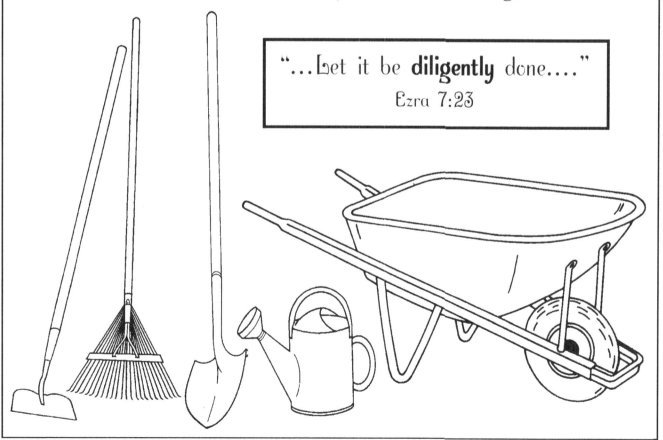

 # Review

Place II - III

(Include Place I if the child can do these problems.)

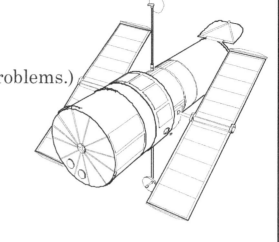

1. What place has four digits?

2. What place has five digits?

3. What place has six digits?

4. Think of these numbers as some of the stars in God's great universe, or as God's chosen people, as you do the following exercises. Tell where the place of these numbers belong. Make a grid for placement in the box below.

62	7,658	34,613	732,551
272	2,271	73,818	318,364
306	13,129	61,832	954,623

5. Write out the number names on a separate piece of paper for the digits in problem four.

6. Make another grid on a separate piece of paper and place the following numbers on it by writing them in digits.

A. five thousand, four hundred forty-seven

B. three thousand, one hundred eighty-two

C. one thousand, three hundred twenty-nine

D. fifty thousand, nine hundred and two

E. sixty-three thousand, six hundred and two

F. twenty-four thousand, eight hundred and sixty-nine

G. two hundred forty thousand, six hundred and one

H. four hundred thirty-nine thousand, five hundred thirty-six

I. seven hundred sixty-three thousand, two hundred thirteen

7. Put commas in the proper places in the numbers to the right. These numbers should remind us of the stars of heaven and God's chosen people.

Reflect
Value
Discuss these thoughts with your teacher.

1. "That which cost little is less valued."
    —*Cervantes* (1605-15)

1715
325
243316
47
9408
65307
948106
38977
26701
84600
2347
336862

2. "We cannot be sure that we have something worth living for unless we are ready to die for it."
    —*Eric Hoffer* (1951)

3. "Those things are dearest to us that have cost us most."
    —*Montaigne* (1580-88)

4. "What we obtain too cheap, we esteem too lightly; it is dearness only that gives everything its value."
    —*Thomas Paine* (1776-83)

5. "The real price of everything, what everything really costs to the man who wants to acquire it, is the toil and trouble of acquiring it."
    —*Adam Smith* (1776)

6. "There is no such thing as absolute value in this world. You can only estimate what a thing is worth to you."
    —*Charles Dudley Warner* (1871)

  # Research

Place Value— Millions/Ten Millions/Hundred Millions/ Billions/Ten Billions/Hundred Billions

"...Repent, and do the first works; or else I will come unto thee quickly, and will remove thy candlestick out of his <u>place</u>, except thou repent."

Revelation 2:5

Lost Sight

Have you ever been star-gaz-ing and lost sight of a star? That experience can remind you of how the Jews, God's <u>chosen</u>, <u>lost</u> <u>sight</u> of the teaching of the ritual service. Each part was to symbolize Jesus Christ, and was full of life and spiri-tual beauty. "But the Jews lost the spiritual life from their ceremonies, and clung to the dead forms." The way was prepared by Satan for them to misunderstand the coming Messiah and His work. Then, when He did come, Israel did not recog-nize Him.

Before and after Jesus came, evidences were multiplied by miracles, examples, ceremonies, and teachings. Still, the Jewish people rejected Him. *"...Repent, and do the first works; or else I will come unto thee quickly, and will remove thy candlestick out of his <u>place</u>, except thou repent"* (Revelation 2:5).

"Things seen are mightier than things heard."
—*Lord Tennyson* (1864)

Israel lost sight of the true meaning of the ritual service

"Only take heed to thyself, and keep thy soul <u>diligently</u>, lest thou forget the things which thine eyes have seen...."
Deuteronomy 4:9

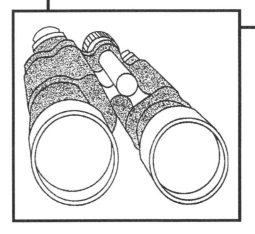

Today, we have even more evidence of Christ's second coming than the Jews did for His first coming. Are we in our <u>place</u> as God's <u>chosen</u> to give the world the message of *"Behold, I come quickly: blessed is he that keepeth the sayings of the prophecy of this book"?* (Revelation 22:7)

Reflect
Sight

"Our sight is the most perfect and most delightful of all our senses. It fills the mind with the largest variety of ideas, converses with its objects at the greatest distance, and continues the longest in action without being tired or satiated with its proper enjoyments."
—*Joseph Addison*
(1711-12)

Digital Value and Place Value

Examples

If a number has seven digits, it is in the millions' <u>place.</u>

If a number has eight digits, it is in the ten millions' <u>place.</u>

If a number has nine digits, it is in the hundred millions' <u>place.</u>

If a number has ten digits, it is in the billions' <u>place.</u>

If a number has eleven digits, it is in the ten billions' <u>place.</u>

If a number has twelve digits, it is in the hundred billions' <u>place.</u>
See page 69.

$$94 = (9 \times 10) + (4 \times 1)$$

digital value   **place value**

Millions

1,000,000
10,000,000
100,000,000

Billions

1,000,000,000
10,000,000,000
100,000,000,000

"The eye obeys exactly the action of the mind."
Emerson (1860)

"The countenance is the portrait of the mind, the eyes are its informers."
—*Cicero*

"Eyes are more accurate witnesses than ears."
—*Heraclitus* (c. 500 B.C.)

You have already learned that every number in the Arabic system has two values which are place and digital value. The digital value is the value given to each digit or symbol, like:

0 - 1 - 2 - 3 - 4 - 5 - 6 - 7 - 8 - 9.

Place value is the value given to the position of a digit, and to its relation to the other digits that make up the number. (See the example on page 56.)

When we move from right to left the value of the place increases. It increases ten times greater for each place to the left. If you want to decrease a digit you would go to the right until finally it would be into the decimals.

As we think of these thoughts, let us learn more about galaxies and how God has chosen (or made a place for) us.

The universe is so large that astronomers use a special measurement called a light year. This is the distance light travels in one year. It equals about 6 million, million miles (9.5 million, million kilometers) or 186,000 miles each second (300,000 kilometers).

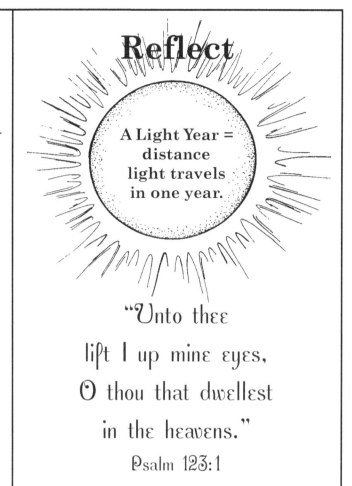

A Light Year = distance light travels in one year.

"Unto thee lift I up mine eyes, O thou that dwellest in the heavens."
Psalm 123:1

It is a blessed condescension on God's part that He permits us to lift up our eyes past the sun, moon, and stars to His glorious high throne; and, that He invites and even commands us so to do. When we are looking to the Lord in hope, it is well to tell Him so in prayer:

Prayer is the burden of a sigh,
The falling of a tear,
The upward glancing of an eye
When none but God is near.

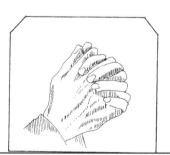

If it were possible to travel in an aircraft at the speed of light, you could go around the Earth seven times in just one second.

Amazing! God has <u>chosen</u> me to be His child! He never loses sight of me. *"Since thou wast precious in my sight, thou hast been honourable, and I have loved thee: therefore will I give men for thee, and people for thy life"* (Isaiah 43:4).

Galaxies do not sit still in space. They spin slowly around and around, just as God's **diligent** children go around about their Father's business.

One complete year is called a galactic year. The Milky Way takes 225,000,000 Earth years to spin once. We would write that to read, two hundred twenty-five million.

There are millions of galaxies and some with billions of stars. No person can count how many stars or galaxies there are, for only God knows. *"He telleth the number of the stars; he calleth them all by their names"* (Psalms 147:4).

The nearest galaxy to our Milky Way galaxy is about two million (2,000,000) light years away.

Reinforce
Seeing Eyes

When the Roman soldiers sacked Jerusalem, not finding any images of gold and silver in the temple, they cried out—"The Jews are worshippers of the clouds!"

Augustine mentions a heathen once saying to him, as he pointed to the sun, to his idol gods, and to various objects about him, "Here are my gods, where is thine?" Augustine answered, "I show you not mine, not because I have no God to show, but because you have not eyes with which to see Him."

All Seeing Eyes

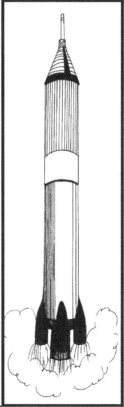

A worldly father said to his son, who attended Sabbath school, and seriously thought of what he heard there. "Carry this parcel to such a place."

"It is the Sabbath," replied the boy.

"Put it into your pocket," replied the father.

"God can see into my pocket," answered the child.

In the Milky Way there are about 40,000,000 (million) stars concentrated in the center. Our solar system lies in one of the arms of the Milky Way. To travel to the center of the Milky Way would take about 33,000 light years. That would be like driving a car from Earth, at 100 miles (161 Kilometers) per hour for 221,000,000 (million) years to get to the center.

Some scientists say there are at least 100,000,000 (million) stars in the Milky Way. They are really not sure how many there are; for only God knows. With this vast universe and worlds without number, still you are the object of His tender care.

Reflect
Precious In My Sight

"Of Christ's relation to His people, there is a beautiful illustration in the laws given to Israel. When through poverty a Hebrew had been forced to part with his patrimony, and to sell himself as a bondservant, the duty of redeeming him and his inheritance fell to the one who was nearest of kin. (See Leviticus 25:25, 47-49; Ruth 2:20.) So the work of redeeming us and our inheritance, lost through sin, fell upon Him who is *'near of kin'* unto us. It was to redeem us that He became our kinsman. Closer than father, mother, brother, friend, or lover is the Lord our Saviour. *'Fear not,'* He says, *'for I have redeemed thee, I have called thee by thy name; thou art mine.' 'Since thou wast precious in <u>my sight</u>, thou hast been honorable, and I have loved thee: therefore will I give men for thee, and people for thy life'* (Isaiah 43:1, 4)."

—*The Desire of Ages 327*

God Made Them All

Milky Way Galaxy

The twinkling stars, God made them all
By His almighty hand.
He holds them that they do not fall,
And bids them move or stand.

How very great that God must be
Who rolls them through the air!
But He's not too high to notice me
Or listen to my prayer!

—*Adapted from Ann Taylor*

How many stars are in the Milky Way?

Our sun is about ninety-three million miles from the Earth!

Review

Place II - III
(Include Place I
if he can do these problems.)

1. The following numbers are to be used to put place values in the grid on the next page.

A. 225,000,000 times the Milky Way spins in one Earth year

B. more than 700,452,654 galaxies
more than 643,411 galaxies
more than 3,198,762 galaxies

C. more than 999,999,999,999 stars
more than 63,411,270,899 stars
more than 1,988,465,432 stars

D. 33,000 light years
221,000,000 years to drive at 100 miles per hour from Earth to the center of the Milky Way

E. 100,000,000 stars in the Milky Way

2. Write out each of the above numbers in the spaces provided on the next page. Be **diligent**!

Reinforce
Eyes and No Eyes

A judicious traveller once went to see one of the greatest wonders of the world. He gazed and gazed, each minute saw more, and might have gone on seeing into the thing for weeks, he said. Two regular tourists walked in, glanced about them, and almost before he could look round they were gone.

—*Sir Arthur Helps*

"He telleth the number
of the stars;
he calleth them all
by their names."
Psalm 147:4

Seeing the Light

"Every shining star which God has placed in the heavens obeys His mandate, and gives its distinctive measure of light to make beautiful the heavens at night; so let every converted soul show the measure of light committed to him; and as it shines forth the light will increase and grow brighter. Give out your light....pour forth your beams mirrored from heaven. O daughter of Zion, *'Arise, shine; for thy light is come, and the glory of the Lord is risen upon thee.'*"

—*4 Bible Commentary* 1153

	Hundred Billions	Ten Billions	Billions	Hundred Millions	Ten Millions	Millions	Hundred Thousands	Ten Thousands	Thousands	Hundreds	Tens	Ones
A.				—	—	—	—	—	—	—	—	—
B.				—	—	—	—	—	—	—	—	—
							—	—	—	—	—	—
				—	—	—	—	—	—	—	—	—
C.	—	—	—	—	—	—	—	—	—	—	—	—
		—	—	—	—	—	—					
			—	—	—	—	—	—	—	—	—	—
D.									—	—	—	—
				—	—	—	—	—	—	—	—	—
E.				—	—	—	—	—	—	—	—	—

Write out the above numbers.

A. _____

_____

B. _____

_____

C._____

_____

D. _____

_____

E. _____

_____

Reflect
We See Light, Harmony, and Beauty in the Heavens

"He telleth the number of the stars." Among the heathen every constellation represented some God. But the Scriptures show Jehovah, not as one of many starry gods, but as the one God of all the stars. He is, too, as He taught His people by Abraham, the God of a firmament of nobler stars. His people are scattered and trodden as the sands of the seashore. But He turns dust and dirt to stars of glory. He will make of every saint a star, and Heaven is His people's sky, where broken-hearted sufferers of earth are glorified into glittering galaxies.

—Hermann Venema

Remainder
The Eyes of the Lord

"Behold, the eye of the Lord is upon them [you] that fear him, upon them that hope in his mercy."

Psalm 33:18

When people lose sight of God they are in darkness. At night, as we look up at the galaxies, we can observe all the lights in the universe, each in its appointed place. Not one inhabitant on any world has ever lost sight of God except the people on planet Earth. This should inspire us not to lose sight of God or His word. Be **diligent** in study!

God never loses sight of you, even though He has a vast universe to care for, for *"the eye of the Lord is upon them* [you]*"* (Psalm 33:18).

"He [Jesus] cares for each one as if there were not another on the face of the earth."*

"He [God] is caring for us every moment; He keeps the living machinery [our bodies] in action; if we were left to run it for one moment, we should die. We are absolutely dependent upon God."**

*The Desire of Ages 480 **Testimonies to Ministers 423

Review
Place II - III
(Include Place I
if the child can do these problems.)
See the Nature lesson,
The Universe and Galaxies
for answers to these questions.

1. Write a definition of millions' place. Write a number as an example. _____

_____

2. Write a definition of billions' place. Write a number as an example. _____

_____

3. What is a light year? _____

_____

Write a light year out in miles per second._____

_____

4. What is a galactic year?

5. How long does it take in earth years for the Milky Way to spin once? Write your answer out on a separate piece of paper.

6. List these numbers in a vertical column, being sure each is in its proper place.

561,326,003; 654,305; 783; 64,860,995; 66,321; 693,285,655; 25; 1,864; 2,671,884.

_____

_____

_____

_____

_____

_____

_____

_____

7. Read the poem above.

"The eye of the Lord is upon them that fear him." That eye of peculiar care is their glory and defense. None can take them unawares, for the celestial watcher foresees the designs of their enemies, and provides against them. Let them fix their eye of faith on Him, and His eye of love will always rest upon them.

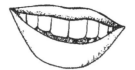

Remind

God not only never loses sight of you, but He watches with great interest how **diligent** you will be in doing each chore. He also watches how you answer and speak to other members of your family.

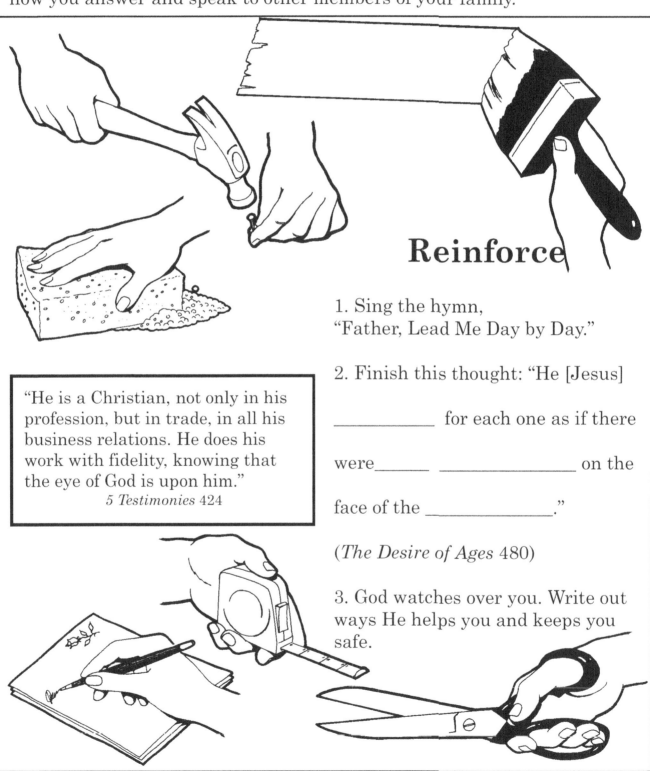

Reinforce

1. Sing the hymn, "Father, Lead Me Day by Day."

2. Finish this thought: "He [Jesus] _____ for each one as if there were_____ _____ on the face of the _____."

(*The Desire of Ages* 480)

3. God watches over you. Write out ways He helps you and keeps you safe.

"He is a Christian, not only in his profession, but in trade, in all his business relations. He does his work with fidelity, knowing that the eye of God is upon him."
5 Testimonies 424

Review
Place I - II - III

1. Have your teacher dictate your spelling words.
   Discuss the spiritual and literal definition
   of these spelling words.

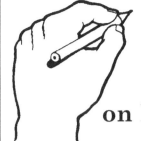

More Review

Ideas for Problems
on Place Value and Written Numbers

Health Lesson II — *The Body*

200 muscles

billions of cells

60,000 miles (96,000 km.) of tubing to carry blood

350 feet per second (105 m./sec.) messages sent to the brain

3 pounds (1.8 kg.) of brain

30 billion nerve cells

70 -100 years a man lives

206 bones

(See an encyclopedia for more information.)

Most people can hear from 20 hertz to 20,000 hertz

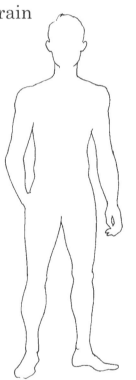

    Dog – 15 hertz to 50,000 hertz

    Bat – 10,000 hertz to 120,000 hertz

    Grasshopper 7,000 hertz to 100,000 hertz
    (hertz = vibrations per second)

Music Lesson II – *How Does Sound Make Music?*

Medium through which Sound Travels	feet/sec.	meters/sec.
Air, 59° F/15° C	1,116	340
Air, 212° F/100° C	1,268	386
Aluminum	16,000	5,000
Brick	11,980	3,650
Distilled water, 77° F/25° C	4,908	1,496
Sea water, 77° F/25° C	5,023	1,531
Glass	14,900	4,540
Steel	17,000	5,200
Wood (maple)	13,480	4,110

Nature Lesson II – *The Universe and Galaxies*

Count words in chapters for larger numbers.

Some stars are about 1,000 times as large as the sun.

The largest stars have a diameter of about 1,000,000,000 miles (16,000,000,000 km).

Blue stars have a surface heat of about 50,000° F. (28,000° C.) - Red stars have a surface heat of about 5,000° F. (2,800° C.).

A light year is 5,880,000,000,000 miles (9,400,000,000,000 km.).

Globular clusters contain from 10,000 to 1,000,000 stars.

The nearest galaxy to the Milky Way is 200,000 light years away.

Elliptical Galaxy   **Spiral Galaxy**

Geography Lesson II – *The Earth*

196,951,000 square miles—earth's area (510,100,000 square kilometers)

5,288,000,000—population of earth (1990)

16,956,000 square miles—Asia—largest continent—(43,917,000 square kilometers)

2,966,150 square miles—Australia—smallest continent—(7,682,300 square kilometers)

8,649,500 square miles - Russia—largest country—(22,402,000 square kilometers)

1/6 square mile—Vatican City—smallest country (0.4 square kilometers)

1,000,000,000—China—most populous country—1990

1,000 citizens—Vatican City—least populous country—1990

29,029 feet above sea level—Mount Everest in Asia—highest point—(399 meters)

36,198 feet below the surface—Challenger Deep—south west of Guam - Mariana Trench—Pacific Ocean (11,033 meters)—deepest point

Language Lesson II – *Your Bible the Word*

3, 566, 480 letters
  773, 742 words
    31, 173 verses
      1, 189 chapters
        929 chapters - Old Testament
        260 chapters - New Testament
        66 books
        39 Old Testament books
        27 New Testament books

Illustration

Place Value

"If the spirit of the ruler rise up against thee,

leave not thy <u>place</u>; for yielding pacifieth great offences."

Ecclesiastes 10:4

This verse is telling us, do not resign your post of duty. Hasty actions reflects a lack of sound judgment. It is better to endure the temporary displeasure then to leave your responsibility.

"Be not hasty

to go out

of his sight...."

Ecclesiastes 8:3

	hundred billions	ten billions	one billions		hundred millions	ten millions	one millions		hundred thousands	ten thousands	one thousands		hundreds	tens	ones
	0	0	0,		0	0	0,		0	0	0,		0	0	0
	Billion				**Million**				**Thousand**				**Units**		

Review
Place I - II - III

1. Israel was unfaithful to the place God gave them to fill. Are you **diligent** in the place God has given you to work?

2. Israel was to demonstrate God's law to the world. The Scriptures were to be lived out in their lives to prepare the earth for Christ's first advent. Are you **diligently** living for Him today?

3. Israel was chosen as a nation out of this world to serve God. Are you chosen?

4. Israel lost sight of their mission to prepare the way for Christ to come to this earth the first time. How is your vision? Do you <u>see</u> He is soon to come? Learn from Israel and prepare the way for Christ's second coming. **Diligence** is the watchword.

Reflect
Diligence

"The industrious bee gives to men of intelligence an example that they would do well to imitate. These insects observe perfect order, and no idler is allowed in the hive. They execute their appointed work with an intelligence and activity that are beyond our comprehension.... The wise man calls our attention to the small things of the earth: *'Go to the ant, thou sluggard; consider her ways, and be wise; which have no guide, overseer, or ruler, provideth her meat in the summer, and gathereth her food in the harvest.' 'The ants are a people not strong, yet they prepare their meat in the summer.'* We may learn from these little teachers a lesson of faithfulness. Should we improve with the same **diligence** the faculties which an all-wise Creator has bestowed upon us, how greatly would our capacities for usefulness be increased. God's eye is upon the smallest of His creatures; does He not, then, regard man formed in His image, and require of him corresponding returns for all the advantages He has given him?"

Child Guidance 59-60

1. God promises His children a place on earth and in heaven.

Isaiah 56:5 – *"Even unto them will I give in mine house and within my walls a place and a name better than of sons and of daughters: I will give them an everlasting name, that shall not be cut off."*

John 14:1-3 – *"Let not your heart be troubled: ye believe in God, believe also in me.*

"In my Father's house are many mansions: if it were not so, I would have told you. I go to prepare a place for you.

"And if I go and prepare a place for you, I will come again, and receive you unto myself; that where I am, there ye may be also."

2. Israel was carried out of their place because of their sins. God finally brought them back to Caanan.

Jeremiah 32:37 – *"Behold, I will gather them out of all countries,* whither I have driven them in mine anger, and in my fury, and in great wrath; and I will bring them again unto this place, and I will cause them to dwell safely."*

3. Jesus was sent and came willingly from heaven to the place called earth. His people did not know Him.

John 1:11 – *"He came unto his own, and his own received him not."*

Matthew 12:6 – *"But I say unto you, That in this place is one greater than the temple."*

4. God called the church of Israel to repent. Today He calls our church to repent or loose the light.

Revelation 2:5 – *"Remember therefore from whence thou art fallen, and repent, and do the first works; or else I will come unto thee quickly, and will remove thy candlestick out of his place, except thou repent."*

5. Do not be like the man who wandered from his place.

Proverbs 27:8 – *"As a bird that wandereth from her nest, so is a man that wandereth from his place."*

6. If others persecute you stay in your place.

Ecclesiastes 10:4 – *"If the spirit of the ruler rise up against thee, leave not thy place; for yielding pacifieth great offences."*

Ecclesiastes 8:3 – *"Be not hasty to go out of his sight: stand not in an evil thing; for he doeth whatsoever pleaseth him."*

7. God's word helps us stay in our place.

Psalm 119:24 – *"Thy testimonies also are my delight, and my counsellors."*

8. We are to work for the Master in our place.

Colossians 3:23 – *"And whatsoever ye do, do it heartily, as to the Lord, and not unto men."*

9. To be in God's will is the best place!

Psalm 90:1 – *"Lord, thou hast been our dwelling place in all generations."*

Heaven will be
a wonderful place
to study mathematics.

Outline of School Program

Age	Grade	Program
Birth through Age 7	Babies Kindergarten and Pre-school	*Family Bible Lessons* (This includes: Bible, Science–Nature, and Character)
Age 8	First Grade	*Family Bible Lessons* (This includes: Bible, Science–Nature, and Character) + Language Program (*Writing and Spelling Road to Reading and Thinking* [WSRRT])
Age 9-14 or 15	Second through Eighth Grade	*The Desire of all Nations* (This includes: Health, Mathematics, Music, Science–Nature, History/Geography/Prophecy, Language, and Voice–Speech) + Continue using WSRRT
Ages 15 or 16-19	Ninth through Twelfth Grade	9 – *Cross and Its Shadow I** + Appropriate Academic Books 10 – *Cross and Its Shadow II** + Appropriate Academic Books 11 – *Daniel the Prophet** + Appropriate Academic Books 12 – *The Seer of Patmos** (Revelation) + Appropriate Academic Books *or you could continue using *The Desire of Ages*
Ages 20-25	College	Apprenticeship

Made in the USA
Monee, IL
21 August 2022

11941357R00066